The Theory and Practice of
Investment
Management
Workbook

THE FRANK J. FABOZZI SERIES

This workbook is the companion, self-study guide to *The Theory and Practice of Investment Management.*

Please visit www.WileyFinance.com for more information.

Fixed Income Securities, Second Edition by Frank J. Fabozzi

Focus on Value: A Corporate and Investor Guide to Wealth Creation by James L. Grant and James A. Abate

Handbook of Global Fixed Income Calculations by Dragomir Krgin

Managing a Corporate Bond Portfolio by Leland E. Crabbe and Frank J. Fabozzi

Real Options and Option-Embedded Securities by William T. Moore

Capital Budgeting: Theory and Practice by Pamela P. Peterson and Frank J. Fabozzi

The Exchange-Traded Funds Manual by Gary L. Gastineau

Professional Perspectives on Fixed Income Portfolio Management, Volume 3 edited by Frank J. Fabozzi

Investing in Emerging Fixed Income Markets edited by Frank J. Fabozzi and Efstathia Pilarinu

Handbook of Alternative Assets by Mark J. P. Anson

The Exchange-Traded Funds Manual by Gary L. Gastineau

The Global Money Markets by Frank J. Fabozzi, Steven V. Mann, and Moorad Choudhry

The Handbook of Financial Instruments edited by Frank J. Fabozzi

Collateralized Debt Obligations: Structures and Analysis by Laurie S. Goodman and Frank J. Fabozzi

Interest Rate, Term Structure, and Valuation Modeling edited by Frank J. Fabozzi

Investment Performance Measurement by Bruce J. Feibel

The Handbook of Equity Style Management edited by T. Daniel Coggin and Frank J. Fabozzi

The Theory and Practice of Investment Management edited by Frank J. Fabozzi and Harry M. Markowitz

Foundations of Economic Value Added: Second Edition by James L. Grant

Financial Management and Analysis: Second Edition by Frank J. Fabozzi and Pamela P. Peterson

Measuring and Controlling Interest Rate and Credit Risk: Second Edition by Frank J. Fabozzi, Steven V. Mann, and Moorad Choudhry

Professional Perspectives on Fixed Income Portfolio Management, Volume 4 edited by Frank J. Fabozzi

The Handbook of European Fixed Income Securities edited by Frank J. Fabozzi and Moorad Choudhry

Credit Derivatives: Instruments, Applications, and Pricing by Mark J.P. Anson, Frank J. Fabozzi, Moorad Choudhry, and Ren-Raw Chen

Handbook of European Structured Financial Products edited by Frank J. Fabozzi and Moorad Choudhry

The Theory and Practice of
Investment
Management
Workbook

*Step-by-Step Exercises and Tests to Help You Master
The Theory and Practice of Investment Management*

FRANK J. FABOZZI

HARRY M. MARKOWITZ

LEONARD KOSTOVETSKY

WILEY

John Wiley & Sons, Inc.

For general information on our other products and services, or technical support, please contact our Customer Care Department within the United States at 800-762-2974, outside the United States at 317-572-3993 or fax 317-572-4002.

Wiley also publishes its books in a variety of electronic formats. Some content that appears in print may not be available in electronic books.

For more information about Wiley products, visit our web site at www.wiley.com.

ISBN: 0-471-48950-6

10 9 8 7 6 5 4 3 2 1

Contents

Questions and Problems

CHAPTER 1

Investment Management

1. What are the five steps in the investment management process?

   a. _____

   b. _____

   c. _____

   d. _____

   e. _____

2. Which of the following investors is *least* likely to have liability-driven investment objectives?

   a. An individual

   b. A savings and loan association

   c. A life insurance company

   d. A pension fund

3. Classify each of the following as a traditional asset class, an alternative investments asset class, a subdivision of a larger asset class, or a benchmark index. If a subdivision, specify the broad asset class under which it is a subdivision and, if a benchmark index, specify the asset class it represents.

a. U.S. government bonds

b. Standard & Poor's 500

c. Hedge funds

d. Real estate

e. U.S. growth stocks

f. Emerging market stocks

g. Mortgage-backed securities

h. Salomon Brothers Broad

For questions 4–7, identify the following statements as *True*, *False*, or *Uncertain*. If *False* or *Uncertain*, explain briefly.

4. The market capitalization of a company with 100 million shares of outstanding stock equals 100 million.

5. It is impossible for small individual investors to obtain exposure to an asset class because they don't have the resources to buy a sufficient number of individual assets comprising that asset class.

6. Investment choices by tax-exempt investors are unaffected by changes in tax policy.

7. As a result of accounting, the performance of pension funds is affected not just by the portfolio performance of the assets, but also by changes in the present value of the liabilities.

8. Which of the following are good reasons for an investor to select a passive portfolio strategy over an active portfolio strategy?

   I. The investor is able to forecast future interest rates with a high degree of accuracy.

  II. The investor believes the market is not fully price-efficient.

 III. The investor wants to maximize return for a certain level of risk.

   a. I only

   b. III only

   c. I and II only

   d. II and III only

   e. I, II, and III

   f. None of the above

9. What are the three critical inputs for the construction of an efficient portfolio, and how can each of these be estimated?

   a. _____

   b. _____

   c. _____

10. Which of the following is *not* a good approach to portfolio construction?

 a. Mean-Variance approach

 b. Multi-Factor risk approach

 c. "Seat-of-the-pants" approach

11. Tracking error is:

 a. The difference between the return on the portfolio and the return on the benchmark index.

 b. The correlation between the return on the portfolio and the return on the benchmark index.

 c. The variance of the difference between the return on the portfolio and the return on the benchmark index.

CHAPTER 2

Portfolio Selection

Use the data in this table to answer questions 1 to 7.

State of the World	Rate of Return for Asset LMN	Rate of Return for Asset OPQ	Probability of Occurrence
1	12%	–2%	0.15
2	7%	6%	0.40
3	4%	4%	0.35
4	0%	25%	0.10

1. Calculate the expected value of the rate of return for each asset.

2. Calculate the variance of the rate of return for each asset. Use this to find the standard deviation of the rate of return for each asset. Which asset is riskier under the Markowitz framework?

3. Calculate the covariance between the returns on assets LMN and OPQ. Use this and your answer in the previous question to find the correlation. Do the two assets generally move together?

Now imagine a portfolio invested 60% in asset LMN and 40% in asset OPQ.

4. What is the expected return on this portfolio? What is the variance of the returns from this portfolio? What is the standard deviation?

5. Is this an efficient portfolio? Try to change the weights to make a portfolio with the same expected return but lower variance.

6. Find the optimal portfolio (the one with lowest variance). This can be done by trial and error, graphically, or by using calculus.

7. Explain why the optimal portfolio contains both assets, even though asset LMN dominates asset OPQ.

For questions 8–11, identify the following statements as *True*, *False*, or *Uncertain*. If *False* or *Uncertain*, explain briefly.

8. Because economists have been unable to measure people's utility functions, mean-variance portfolio theory is inherently flawed and unusable.

9. If two assets have a correlation of –1, it may be possible to construct a risk-free (zero-variance) portfolio even when both assets are risky (have a positive variance).

10. It is possible for the beta of a portfolio (β_p) to be greater than the betas of all of the constituents even if the portfolio weights are between 0 and 1.

11. All points on the same indifference curve are at the same level of risk for a given investor.

12. Which of the following might cause two investors to have different optimal portfolios?

  I. Different risk and return preferences
 II. Different expectations of the return from a certain asset
III. Different expectations of the covariance between two assets

   a. I only

   b. II only

   c. II and III only

   d. I, II, and III

   e. None of the above

13. Which of the following is a valid criticism of the use of variance as a measure of risk?

  I. It doesn't take into account the asymmetry of returns around the mean.
 II. It is difficult to estimate from historical data.
III. It is difficult to calculate for a portfolio of a large number of securities.
IV. The semivariance is easier to compute and utilize.

   a. I only

   b. I and IV only

   c. I, III, and IV only

   d. III and IV only

   e. I, II, III, and IV

14. Which one of the following assets is referred to as "risk-free"?

   a. Stock that you're planning to sell next week

   b. U.S. 10-year Treasury note

   c. Foreign government short-term obligation

   d. U.S. 3-month T-bill

Use the following graph to answer questions 15–17.

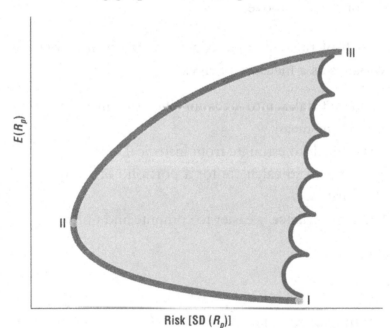

Risk [SD (R_p)]

15. What is the feasible set of portfolios on this graph?

16. What is the Markowitz efficient frontier on this graph?

17. Do you have enough information to determine the optimal portfolio? If not, what do you need?

18. The Homogeneous Expectations Assumption is defined as the assumption that:

a. All investors have the same risk-return preferences.

b. All investors have the same values for the three critical inputs of expected returns, variances, and covariances for all risky assets.

c. All investors seek to achieve the highest expected return at a given level of risk.

d. All investors are exactly identical.

CHAPTER 3

Applying Mean-Variance Analysis

Use the data in the following table to answer questions 1–4.

Parameter	Index ABC	Index DEF	Index GHI
Annualized Return (1995–1998)	5.7%	16.2%	26.5%
Annualized Return (1999–2002)	5.9%	−7.5%	3.3%
Annualized S.D. (1995–1998)	2.8%	12.2%	13.9%
Annualized S.D. (1999–2002)	2.9%	19.2%	4.9%

1. If you were predicting the future expected return and standard deviation using historical data, for which index would you have the most confidence in your prediction? Why?

2. What additional information would probably cause you to decide to decrease the weight of Index DEF in your portfolio?

   I. Index DEF represents equities from a country that underwent a severe recession from 1999 to 2002. This recession has recently ended.

  II. Indexes ABC and GHI represent asset classes with a high exposure to fixed income while DEF has high exposure to equity.

 III. Prior to 1995, Index GHI had an average yearly return of 2.6% with a standard deviation of 14.6%.

   a. I only

   b. I and III only

   c. II and III only

   d. I, II, and III

   e. None of the Above

3. What is the best estimate of Index GHI's return in 2003?

   a. 26.5%

   b. 3.3%

   c. 14.9%

   d. All of the above are valid estimates because there is no right answer for the best estimate.

4. What are three methods that you can use to deal with the instability of parameters like those in Index DEF and Index GHI?

a. _____

b. _____

c. _____

5. Calculate the monthly rate of return on a stock that appreciated in price from $20 to $22 during the month. What assumptions do you have to make for your calculation to be valid?

6. Assume you make the following two estimates:

I. Using monthly data from 1926–2003, you estimate that the expected annualized return on a 30-day U.S. Treasury bill is 3%.

II. Using monthly data from 1996–2003, you estimate that the expected annualized return on the Algerian stock market is 22%.

Which is likely to be a better estimate? List several reasons.

Use the data in the following table to answer questions 7–9.

Asset Class	Portfolio X	Portfolio X′	Portfolio X″
U.S. Fixed Income	63.1%	44.3%	47.9%
U.S. Equity	36.9%	30.0%	42.1%
International Equity	—	25.7%	10%
Expected Return	9.71%	10.55%	10.22%
Standard Deviation	8%	8%	8%

Portfolio X is the efficient 2-asset portfolio with 8% standard deviation.
Portfolio X′ is the efficient 3-asset portfolio with 8% standard deviation
Portfolio X″ is the efficient 3-asset portfolio with 8% standard deviation and a 10% maximum constraint on international equity.

7. Which of the three portfolios is riskiest under the Markowitz framework?

8. Give a possible reason for an investor to choose Portfolio X″ instead of Portfolio X′. What is the trade-off here?

9. If you added a fourth asset class, which of the following could be the expected return of an efficient (4-asset) portfolio with 8% standard deviation and no constraints?

   a. 9.71%

   b. 10.22%

   c. 11.32%

10. List four concerns that must be taken into account when implementing a portfolio using active strategies.

    a. _____

    b. _____

    c. _____

    d. _____

For questions 11–12, identify the following statements as *True*, *False*, or *Uncertain*. If *False* or *Uncertain*, explain briefly.

11. It's always better to rebalance quarterly rather than yearly, and even better to rebalance monthly so that the asset weights don't have time to deviate from those in the optimal portfolio.

12. There is no right index to implement a passive strategy because all indexes have their advantages and disadvantages.

CHAPTER 4

Asset Pricing Models

1. What is the risk premium on short-term U.S. government obligations? What is the variance of the expected returns on these assets?

For questions 2–3, assume a certain asset has a beta of 2 and the risk premium of the market portfolio is 5%. The risk-free rate is 6%.

2. What is the risk premium of this asset under the Capital Asset Pricing Model (CAPM)?

3. What is the expected return of this asset under the CAPM?

4. What is the sole source of risk in the CAPM? Is it systematic or not?

5. Which of the following, if true, would undermine the validity of the Capital Asset Pricing Model?

I. A number of investors form their portfolio by intuition alone, and thus avoid using Markowitz portfolio selection.

II. It is difficult to borrow or lend large sums of money because of government anti-usury laws.

III. Analyst A has a buy rating on the stock of company X and believes it will succeed and appreciate in price. Analyst B has a sell rating on that stock and believes the company will go out of business in six months.

a. I only

b. I and II only

c. II and III only

d. I and III only

e. I, II, and III

6. The Capital Market Line (CML):

I. is a straight line tangent to the efficient frontier at the market portfolio.
II. is the set of all portfolios with beta equal to 1.
III. has a risk premium equal to the beta of portfolio M.

   a. I only

   b. I and II only

   c. I and III only

   d. I, II, and III

   e. None of the above

For questions 7–9, identify the following statements as *True*, *False*, or *Uncertain*. If *False* or *Uncertain*, explain briefly.

7. The Sharpe measure of the market portfolio is equal to the equilibrium market price of risk.

8. The Security Market Line (SML) gives the required return for an asset for its level of systematic risk.

9. The Treynor, Sharpe, and Jensen measures of a portfolio are equally useful regardless of whether the portfolio is well diversified.

Use the data in the following table to answer questions 10–13.

Parameter	Portfolio A	Portfolio B
Mean return	11%	15%
Standard deviation	30%	25%
Beta	1.25	2.5
Jensen measure	1%	0%
Market premium	4%	4%
Risk-free rate	5%	5%

10. Which portfolio is better according to the Treynor measure? Which is better according to the Sharpe measure? Which is better according to the Jensen measure? Does it matter which measure you use?

11. Which portfolio would be dominant under the Markowitz mean-variance framework? Why does this conflict with two of your answers in question 10?

12. Which portfolio has higher nonsystematic risk?

13. What is the expected market return as predicted by the CAPM model?

14. What are two important results of empirical studies questioning the validity of the CAPM? How does Richard Roll assess these studies?

15. Identify and explain two modifications of the CAPM.

a. _____

b. _____

16. Explain the difference between the beta in the market model and the beta in the CAPM. What role does the confusion between these two betas play in the arguments over the validity of the CAPM?

Use the data in the following table to answer questions 17–19.

Asset	Price per share	Payoff in State 1 per share	Payoff in State 2 per share
A	$2.20	$4	$6
B	$2	$5	$5
C	$30	$55	$65

17. What is the payoff in state 1 if you own 5 shares of asset A and 7 shares of asset B? What is the payoff in state 2 from this portfolio?

18. How much does it cost to buy the portfolio in question 17?

19. Is there an arbitrage opportunity? If yes, explain how you would exploit it.

Use the data in the following table to answer question 20. Assume you know that the risk premium on factor 1 is 5%, the risk premium on factor 2 is 4%, and the risk premium on factor 3 is 9%. The risk-free rate is 3%.

Parameter	Portfolio A	Portfolio B	Portfolio C
Beta on factor 1	0.7	0.6	0.3
Beta on factor 2	0.8	1.3	0.0
Beta on factor 3	0.1	1.1	1.7

20. What is the expected return on each of the three portfolios according to Arbitrage Pricing Theory?

21. List three classes of popular multi-factor risk models.

a. _____

b. _____

c. _____

CHAPTER 5

Calculating Investment Returns

1. Identify five reasons why investors generally prefer percentage rates of return instead of absolute dollar returns.

a. _____

b. _____

c. _____

d. _____

e. _____

2. Take an investor who buys a stock for $10 and sells it in a month for $12. What is the monthly rate of return expressed as a percentage?

3. Now take an investor who owned this stock for a long time. At the beginning of the month, the market value of the stock was $10 and at the end of the month, the market value rose to $12. What is the monthly rate of return expressed as a percentage?

4. What is the difference between questions 2 and 3?

5. Now let's assume for question 3 that there was also a cash dividend of $1 paid out and reinvested at the end of the month. How does this affect the rate of return?

6. What if the investor in the previous question didn't reinvest his or her dividend and also realized a gain of $2. How does this change the rate of return you calculated in question 5?

7. Which of the following transactions is *not* a cash flow?

   a. An investor taking money out of a brokerage account

   b. A mutual fund receiving a check from an investor to purchase shares in the fund

   c. An increase in market value of inventory as a result of a spike in the price of the goods in the inventory

   d. The U.S. government sending out a tax rebate check

8. For which of the following calculations do we need to know the timing of cash flows made during the period we are examining?

   I. Return on Investment (ROI)

II. Money-weighted Return (MWR)

III. Time-weighted Return (TWR)

    a. I only

    b. II only

    c. II and III only

    d. I and III only

    e. I, II, and III

Use the data in the following table to answer questions 9–13.

Date	Transaction
Jan. 1	Initial investment = $1000
Mar. 31—Valuation	Market value = $800
Apr. 1	Additional investment = $100
May 31—Valuation	Market value = $1200
Jun. 1	Additional investment = $300
Oct. 31—Valuation	Market value = $1700
Nov. 1	Withdrawal = $400
Dec. 31—Valuation	Market value = $1000

9. Calculate the ROI for this portfolio.

10. What is the equation that we can use to solve for the IRR of this portfolio? (Hint: Plugging in 0% for IRR should equalize the two sides.)

11. Calculate the Modified Dietz Return for this portfolio.

12. Calculate the TWR for this portfolio.

13. Why is the TWR lower than all the other returns calculated in questions 9–11? What does this say about the manager's asset allocation decisions? What does it say about the investor's decisions in the timing of cash flows?

14. Compare and contrast IRR and TWR as tools to measure investment performance. What are the advantages and disadvantages of each?

The return in year 1 on a portfolio is 10%, the return in year 2 on a portfolio is 15%, and the return in year 3 on that portfolio is 40%. Use this data to answer questions 15–17.

15. What is the cumulative return of this portfolio over three years?

16. What is the average (arithmetic mean) yearly return of this portfolio?

17. What is the geometric mean yearly return of this portfolio?

18. What is the major problem of using the arithmetic mean return?

a. It overstates the actual return when used for compounding.

b. It is a biased estimator of the expected return in the future.

c. It is always smaller than the geometric mean.

d. It is difficult to calculate.

19. Calculate the annualized return on an investment that returned 20% over 18 months.

CHAPTER 6

Common Stock Markets, Trading Arrangements, and Trading Costs

1. Match the following terms related to equities from Chapter 6 with their descriptions.

Terms

1. Preferred stock

2. Odd lots

3. Soft dollars

4. Impact costs

5. American Depository Receipts

6. Wilshire 4500

7. NASD

8. Crossing networks

9. SuperDot

Descriptions

a. A securities industry self-regulatory organization that owns and operates the largest OTC market in the United States

b. Allow a foreign corporation's equity to be traded on United States stock markets

c. Used to obtain services such as research or other services without charge in exchange for routing a prespecified amount of orders through a certain broker-dealer

d. Is entitled to priority over common stock in the distribution of earnings, dividends, and so forth

e. Contains stocks whose capitalization is smaller than those in the S&P500

f. Electronic delivery system linking NYSE member firms around the world directly to the specialist's post on the trading floor

g. An order to buy 56 shares of a stock would be an example

h. Systems that match buyers and sellers directly via computers

i. Result from changes in the market price due to imbalances arising from a trade

2. Which of the following is an example of stock trading in the third market?

a. Trading Microsoft shares between two mutual funds over Instinet

b. Trading General Electric shares on the New York Stock Exchange

c. Trading General Electric shares on the over-the-counter market

d. Trading of Pink Sheet stocks

3. Which of the following are characteristics of OTC markets?

I. Small-cap stocks are most commonly traded here.
II. Fewer stocks are traded than on the NYSE.
III. There is no central trading floor.

a. I and III only

b. II and III only

c. III only

d. I, II, and III

e. None of the above

4. Which of the following is true about NYSE specialists?

I. There is only one specialist at each "post" on the trading floor.
II. There is only one specialist for the common stock of each company.
III. Specialists have exclusive access to the limit order book giving them an advantage over other traders.

IV. As principals, specialists are required to maintain a fair and orderly market.

    a. I, III, and IV only

    b. II and IV only

    c. III and IV only

    d. II, III, and IV only

    e. I, II, III, and IV

    f. None of the above

5. Which of the following is *not* an advantage of Electronic Communications Networks?

    a. Transparency through access to what is essentially a limit order book

    b. Effective means of executing large orders

    c. Minimizing transaction costs

    d. Easier to subscribe to ECN than to get a seat on the NYSE

6. Which of the following is usually *not* a role of NYSE specialists?

   a. Assuring a reasonable price at the opening including participation if there is a supply-demand imbalance

   b. To discontinue trading in a stock if it is impossible to maintain a fair and orderly market

   c. Trading for their own accounts where they see an opportunity for a profit

   d. Trading against the market trend to maintain liquidity and continuity in the price of the stock

7. Exchanges are different from OTC markets in that they:

   I. Have more stringent requirements in order to get listed.
   II. Only allow members with seats to trade securities directly on the floor.
   III. Operate as auction markets with a specialist acting as auctioneer.

   a. I only

   b. I and II only

   c. II and III only

   d. I and III only

   e. I, II, and III

8. Classify each of the following as an exchange, an OTC Market, an ECN, or a crossing network. One of these belongs to more than one class.

    a. Instinet

    b. Pink Sheets

    c. ITG Posit

d. AMEX

e. Archipelago

f. Nasdaq

9. Classify each of the following as a market order, a limit order, a stop order, stop-limit order, market if touched order, or a fill or kill order. The current price of stock X is $30.

a. An order to sell stock X only if the price falls to or below $20.

b. An order to sell stock X only at $40 or above.

c. An order to sell stock X at the best price available in the market.

d. An order to sell stock X at or above $20 only after the price falls to or below $20.

e. An order to sell stock X only at $30.50 or above; it is canceled if it is not immediately executed.

f. An order to sell stock X at the best available price only if the price reaches or exceeds $40.

10. What are the disadvantages of each of the following orders?

a. market order

b. limit order

c. stop order

Assume Mrs. Smith wants to invest in stock XYZ whose current market price is $10. Answer questions 11–14 regarding her possible opportunities.

11. She has $1,000 to invest. How many shares of XYZ can she buy without using margin? What is her return (on equity) if the stock rises to $15?

12. Assume the initial margin requirement is 1/3 (or 33.3%). Also, assume that the broker charges 5% for the margin loan. What is the largest number of shares that Mrs. Smith can buy? What would be her return (on equity) if she borrows the maximum amount and the stock again rises to $15?

13. Assume she bought on margin as in question 12 and the stock price instead fell to $7. What would be her remaining equity if she sold out?

14. Assume that instead of selling out as in question 13, she wants to stay invested in stock XYZ. How much extra cash must she add to the account to pay off the previous interest payment and to increase her equity to meet a 20% maintenance margin requirement?

15. Short sales require:

I. That the current price of the stock is higher or unchanged from the trade price that immediately preceded it.
II. That the investor already owns the shares to be sold short.
III. That the proceeds of the sale be either reinvested in the stock market or removed from the account.

   a. I only

   b. I and II only

   c. I and III only

   d. II and III only

   e. I, II, and III

   f. None of the above

16. Which of the following are examples of implicit trading costs?

  I. Taxes paid on stock dividends
 II. Not making a trade because a limit order is never executed
III. Large trades moving the price before they are fully executed

  a. I only

  b. II only

  c. I and III only

  d. II and III only

  e. I, II, and III

17. When were price limits first used in the stock market? Why are they needed?

For questions 18–21, identify the following statements as *True*, *False*, or *Uncertain*. If *False* or *Uncertain*, explain briefly.

18. All commissions for stock market trades have declined consistently since 1975.

19. Soft dollar trades can be disadvantageous for investors because they are often unable to obtain the lowest possible commissions.

20. Payments for order flow are good for retail investors because some of the payment is returned to the customer in the form of lower commissions.

21. One major disadvantage of pretrade benchmarks is that they are difficult to measure.

22. Which of the following is *not* true about trading costs?

    a. As a result of discount brokers, most implicit costs have been declining over the last three decades.

    b. There is a consensus that implicit trading costs are significant and must not be ignored.

    c. There is little agreement on the best way of measuring implicit trading costs.

    d. They can be classified into four groups: commissions, impact, timing, and opportunity costs.

23. Identify three major differences between retail stock trading and institutional trading.

    a. _____

    b. _____

    c. _____

24. Which of the following statements is true about program trades?

    a. They are more expensive than performing individual trades one at a time.

    b. Blind baskets can be used to avoid frontrunning.

    c. Agency program trades are useful because they minimize implicit transaction costs.

    d. Agency incentive agreements allow the investor to know the commission and execution price which minimizes risk.

25. How can brokerage firms protect themselves when they don't know the exact portfolio that they are assigned to program trade (blind baskets)?

26. What are two functions performed by stock market indicators?

    a. _____

    b. _____

27. Identify whether each of the following statements pertains to the Dow Jones Industrial Average, the S&P 500 Index,

the Nasdaq Composite, or the Wilshire 5,000. Each statement may pertain to more than one indicator.

a. Represents stocks traded on a certain exchange or OTC market

b. Is a market-weighted index

c. Is constructed from 30 of the largest blue-chip companies

d. Is the most comprehensive index

e. Members subjectively chosen by organizations

28. Which of the following is true about global diversification?

I. The lower the correlation among markets of different countries, the better it can be achieved.
II. Its benefits have been diminished by globalization in the late twentieth century, which has made countries interdependent.
III. Companies in global sectors do not contribute as much to global diversification.

a. III only

b. I and II only

c. I and III only

d. II and III only

e. I, II, and III

29. Which of the following factors, if true, would lead to higher correlations among various countries' stock markets?

   I. "Flight to quality" during financial crises
   II. Stricter capital flow restrictions
   III. Higher international trade

   a. I only

   b. III only

   c. I and II only

   d. I and III only

   e. II and III only

   f. I, II, and III

30. Give three reasons why Global Depositary Receipts are useful for both corporations and investors.

   a. _____

   b. _____

   c. _____

CHAPTER 7

Tracking Error and Common Stock Portfolio Management

Use the data in the following table to answer questions 1–5.

Performance	Manager A	Manager B	Benchmark
Year 1	12%	12%	10%
Year 2	10%	15%	8%
Year 3	9%	4%	7%

1. What is the active return for each manager in each of the three years?

2. What is the alpha of each manager over the three years?

3. Use a spreadsheet program or the formulas in Chapter 2 to calculate the backward-looking tracking error of each manager.

4. What is the information ratio of each manager? Which manager is doing a better job in creating excess return?

5. If Manager B only controls 10% of Portfolio X while the other 90% of Portfolio X is indexed, what is the tracking error of this portfolio?

6. Which of the following statements are true concerning forward-looking tracking error?

I. It is also called ex-post tracking error.
II. It is useful in risk control and portfolio construction because the manager can tweak his or her strategy and check the future outcome.
III. It is equal to the backward-looking tracking error which will be calculated in one year.

   a. II only

   b. III only

   c. I and II only

   d. II and III only

   e. I, II, and III only

7. We know that the variance of quarterly active returns for a portfolio is 25%. What does this information imply?

   a. The information ratio is greater than zero.

   b. The annual tracking error is 25%.

   c. The annual tracking error is 10%.

   d. The annual tracking error is 5%.

   e. The alpha is 5%.

8. Which of the following changes would probably cause the tracking error of a portfolio to increase?

I. Include more stocks from the benchmark index in the portfolio.
II. The benchmark index becomes less volatile.
III. The portfolio beta falls from 1.1 to 1.

a. I only

b. III only

c. I and II only

d. I and III only

e. I, II, and III

f. None of the above

9. Which of the following changes would probably cause the tracking error of a portfolio that tracks the S&P500 to decrease?

a. Including fewer stocks from the index in the portfolio.

b. Including more small-cap stocks in the portfolio

c. Including a good blend of value and growth stocks in the portfolio

d. Making more bets on sectors that aren't represented in the index

e. None of the above

10. Portfolio Z had a 5% exposure to the telecommunica-
    tions sector while the S&P500 had a 9% exposure to this
    sector. Changing the exposure from 5% to 8% causes the
    tracking error (with respect to the S&P500) to drop from
    15% to 9%. What is the marginal contribution of this
    sector?

11. If the exposure increased again from 8% to 10%, would
    you expect the tracking error to fall to 5%? Why or why
    not?

12. What are three possible solutions if a CIO sees that one of the asset class portfolio managers is experiencing growing tracking error without providing higher alpha?

a. _____

b. _____

c. _____

Common Stock Portfolio Management Strategies

For questions 1–3, identify the following statements as *True*, *False*, or *Uncertain*. If *False* or *Uncertain*, explain briefly.

1. Investment management is a simple process that involves sequentially following five fundamental steps.

2. Empirical research suggests that the stock market is efficient.

3. Insider trading suggests that the market is not strong-form efficient.

4. What are the two measures that allow us to distinguish between an actively managed portfolio and a passively managed portfolio?

   a. _____

   b. _____

5. Which of the following statements is *least* likely to be true about a passively managed portfolio?

   a. It has an alpha of 0%.

   b. It has a tracking error of 0%.

   c. Its owner believes that the stock market is not very efficient.

   d. It is implemented through the capitalization approach to indexing.

6. Constructing a portfolio whose risk profile is similar but not identical to that of a market benchmark is called:

   a. Style management

   b. A buy-and-hold strategy

   c. Technical analysis

   d. Enhanced indexing

7. Which of the following statements concerning value managers is true?

I. A subgroup of them looks at companies with higher than average dividend yields.

II. They concentrate on relative prices instead of earnings growth.

III. They buy stocks whose P/B ratios are expected to fall.

   a. I only

   b. II only

   c. I and II only

   d. I and III only

   e. I, II, and III

8. List and define the three substyles of value management.

   a. _____

   b. _____

   c. _____

9. List and define the two substyles of growth management.

   a. _____

   b. _____

10. Which of the following is true about the Morningstar system of classifying mutual funds?

   I. The amount of money in the mutual fund is one of the two variables used for classification.
   II. Style is determined by using the P/B and P/E ratios of the fund's holdings.
   III. There are a total of 15 possible classifications under the Morningstar system.

   a. I only

   b. II only

   c. I and II only

   d. I and III only

   e. I, II, and III

11. Describe four methods of implementing an indexing strategy.

   a. _____

   b. _____

   c. _____

   d. _____

12. Which of the following best describes the top-down approach to active investing?

    a. Managing money directly instead of allowing the market indexes to dictate asset allocation decisions

    b. Buying a greater proportion of large-cap stocks than small-cap stocks

    c. Focusing on asset allocation and letting other managers manage each individual asset class

    d. Establishing which sectors will do best in the future and then deciding which specific stocks are best for gaining exposure to those sectors

13. Identify each of the following analyses as belonging to the field of technical analysis, fundamental analysis, both, or neither.

    a. Visiting a factory to gauge the prospects of the firm's products

    b. Buying after a sharp decline caused by negative news

    c. Using the EVA (Economic Value Added) to determine which stocks to buy and which to sell short

    d. Selling short because of the belief that the economy is about to collapse

    e. Selling short because of the belief that a specific company may soon declare bankruptcy

    f. Using nonlinear dynamic models

14. Which of the following is implied by the Fundamental Law of Active Management?

    I. It is possible for a manager with less skill to produce a better information ratio than a more skilled manager.
   II. A high level of skill is necessary to produce a high information ratio in an efficient market.
  III. For any constant level of reward/risk, there is an inverse relationship (trade-off) between depth and breadth.

    a. II only

    b. I and II only

    c. II and III only

    d. I and III only

    e. I, II, and III

15. Which of the following ratios is most likely to be used by a technical analyst?

    a. Price-to-earnings ratio (P/E)

    b. Price-to-book ratio (P/B)

    c. Dividend Yield (D/P)

    d. Short Interest Ratio

16. What is likely the main reason that 80% of active managers have been unable to outperform a single indexing strategy?

   a. The number of investment opportunities that can be researched is limited by time and cost.

   b. Most active managers don't have the skill to outperform the market.

   c. Passive managers are usually more skilled than active managers.

   d. Active managers have many different benchmarks.

CHAPTER 9

Traditional Fundamental Analysis I: Sources of Information

1. List six ways to obtain information on a firm's earnings in the previous fiscal year.

   a. _____

   b. _____

   c. _____

   d. _____

   e. _____

   f. _____

2. What are the four major functions of the SEC?

a. _____

b. _____

c. _____

d. _____

3. The MDA (Management Discussion and Analysis):

  I. Is usually issued as an appendix to the annual statement to shareholders.
  II. Is a mandatory part of the 10-K filing.
III. Helps explain the company's numerical financial results.

a. II only

b. III only

c. I and III only

d. II and III only

e. I, II, and III

4. Which of the following would probably *not* be found in a proxy statement?

a. The CEO's compensation package

b. The company's plans for future mergers and acquisitions

c. Information about the company's current auditor

d. Information about possible managerial conflicts-of-interest

5. In response to which of the following events is a company *required* to make an 8-K filing?

a. Bankruptcy

b. New product boosting earnings

c. Retirement of a member of the Board of Directors

d. New format for the Annual Report

6. Which of the following documents is *least* likely to be taken seriously by financial analysts?

a. 10-K SEC filing

b. Annual Report to shareholders

c. Letter to shareholders

d. Proxy statement

7. What are three important issues to be aware of in analyzing data from companies' financial statements?

a. _____

b. _____

c. _____

8. Which of the following statements are *True* concerning industry data?

I. NAICS is a simple unambiguous system for classifying companies by industry.

II. There are multiple government and financial service company sources that provide data for specific industries.

III. One must be careful when interpreting industry statistics.

a. I only

b. III only

c. I and II only

d. II and III only

e. I, II, and III

9. What is a major problem with using fundamental multi-factor risk models?

a. They can produce flawed results if not enough time is spent on choosing the correct inputs.

b. Their output is difficult to implement in the real world.

c. They contain too many subjective factors and not enough objective factors.

d. They are not as effective as technical models.

For questions 10–11, identify the following statements as *True*, *False*, or *Uncertain*. If *False* or *Uncertain*, explain briefly.

10. Interviews with company representatives are used to find out basic information about the company.

11. Joint ventures where the corporation doesn't have a controlling interest can be kept off the balance sheet.

CHAPTER 10

Traditional Fundamental Analysis II: Financial Ratio Analysis

1. Classify each of the following measures as a coverage ratio, return ratio, turnover ratio, component percentage, or none of the above.

   a. Net working capital

   b. Basic earning power

c. Quick ratio

d. Debt-to-assets ratio

e. Operating cycle

f. Net profit margin

g. Accounts receivable turnover ratio

Use the data in the following table to answer questions 2–4.

Parameter	Company D
Total Sales	$30,000
Cost of Goods Sold	$16,000
Other Operating Expenses	$4,000
Interest	$1,000
Taxes	$2,000

2. Calculate the gross profit margin, the operating profit margin, and the net profit margin of Company D.

3. If Company D has assets of $50,000, what is its basic earning power? What is its return on assets?

4. Which of the following are *not* implied by the table and the answers to questions 2 and 3?

  I. The total asset turnover ratio of the company is 0.6.
 II. Shareholders earn 14% on their investments in the firm.
III. For every dollar in sales, Company D spends 10 cents on financing and taxes.

  a. I only

  b. II only

  c. I and II only

  d. I and III only

  e. I, II, and III

5. Which of the following is a component of basic earning power under the Du Pont system?

   a. Net profit margin

   b. Operating profit margin

   c. Tax retention

   d. Current ratio

Use the data in the following table as well as in the previous table to answer questions 6–9.

Parameter	Company D
Inventory on hand	$5,000
Accounts receivable	$2,000
Current assets	$20,000
Current liabilities	$15,000

6. Assuming that half of all sales are on credit, calculate the average day's credit sales. Also, calculate the average day's cost of goods sold.

7. Calculate the number of days of inventory and the number of days of credit.

8. What is the operating cycle of Company D? If its number of days of payables is 30, what is its net operating cycle?

9. Which of the following are *true* about Company D?

I. Its quick ratio is 4/3.
II. Its net working capital-to-sales ratio is 17% (rounded to the nearest whole number).
III. Its current ratio is 4/3.

a. II only

b. III only

c. I and III

d. II and III

e. I, II, and III

10. What do activity ratios measure? Give four examples. What information are we unable to gain from these ratios?

a. _____

b. _____

c. _____

d. _____

11. Which of the following is true of the *market* value of equity?

a. It consists of the accumulative earnings of the firm since it was first incorporated, less any stock repurchased by the firm.

b. It is the value for shareholders equity that one would find on the company's balance sheet.

c. It is usually used as an input for financial ratio analysis including the debt-to-equity ratio and return on equity.

d. It is the value of the company as perceived by investors.

12. Which of the following elements from the income state-
    ment are *not* necessary to calculate the fixed charge cover-
    age ratio?

    a. Tax expenses

    b. Interest expenses

    c. Lease expenses

    d. EBIT

13. Which of the following may limit the usefulness of finan-
    cial ratio analysis?

     I. Market values for financial variables deviate greatly from
        book values.
    II. There is no data for previous time periods.
   III. The company is too diversified (operates in too many sec-
        tors) to find a suitable benchmark.

    a. I only

    b. II only

    c. I and II only

    d. II and III only

    e. I, II, and III

14. Which of the following are likely to be *true* about a company that has an extraordinarily high current ratio?

   I. The company has very little debt.
  II. The company is very liquid and can easily meet its financial obligations.
 III. The company is tying up its assets in low-earning assets, which might be reducing its potential profitability.

   a. I only

   b. II only

   c. I and II only

   d. II and III only

   e. I, II, and III

15. Which of the following would you find *most* troubling about a large banking firm? Why? (All numbers are in comparison to an average firm, not an average firm in the industry.)

   a. It has a high debt-to-equity ratio.

   b. It has a very high inventory turnover ratio.

   c. It has a low return on equity.

   d. It has a low return on assets.

16. What's the likely reason behind the decreasing return on equity from Wal-Mart Stores?

    a. Lower inventory turnover

    b. A lower equity multiplier

    c. A higher current ratio

    d. Increased competition squeezing profit margins

17. Which of the following can be reasonably concluded from the Wal-Mart case study?

    a. Wal-Mart is more efficient than its competitors which allows it to have a better return on equity.

    b. Wal-Mart's declining current ratio suggests that it may go bankrupt.

    c. As a result of its superior turnover ratios, its grocery business is likely to put other grocery chains out of business.

18. What is the *most* important lesson from the Wal-Mart case study?

    a. Wal-Mart is one of the best-run companies in the United States.

    b. It is important to compare financial ratios of a company to other companies in the industry and across time in order to make valid conclusions about its future. Simply looking at the numbers in isolation brings very little benefit.

c. It is not always easy and straightforward how to calculate financial ratios for real companies, because companies report their financial data in many different ways.

d. It is important to compare how a company does in good and bad economic times before deciding whether to invest in it.

Traditional Fundamental Analysis III: Earnings Analysis, Cash Analysis, Dividends, and Dividend Discount Models

1. What are four different types of earnings that analysts often look at in determining the performance of a company?

    a. _____

    b. _____

    c. _____

    d. _____

For questions 2–5, identify the following statements as *True*, *False*, or *Uncertain*. If *False* or *Uncertain*, explain briefly.

2. Companies can use legal accounting methods to manipulate earnings in order to meet or exceed analysts' expectations.

3. Positive earnings surprises lead to smaller price adjustments (upward) than negative earnings surprises (downward).

4. Stock returns are correlated with earnings.

5. Positive earnings surprises always lead to a substantial upward revision in the price.

6. Diluted earnings per share:

a. Uses gross profits for earnings.

b. Uses EBITDA for earnings.

    c. Adjusts the number of shares outstanding for securities-like options and convertible debts that can potentially create more shares.

    d. Is usually not reported in financial statements.

7. Which of the following statements concerning earnings analysis are supported by most research?

    I. Complex statistical models that forecast earnings do a much better job than naive extrapolative statistical models.
   II. Naive statistical models do about as good a job in predicting earnings as analysts.
  III. The consensus earnings forecast is a nonbiased predictor of the actual earnings number.

    a. II only

    b. III only

    c. I and II only

    d. I and III only

    e. I, II, and III

8. Which of the following tells why the consensus earnings forecast is not the best estimator of actual earnings?

    I. Analysts make forecasts at different times so they shouldn't all be given equal weight when averaging.
   II. Analysts are usually overly optimistic.

III. The best financial analysts don't make their forecasts public.

   a. I only

   b. II only

   c. I and II only

   d. II and III only

   e. I, II, and III

Use the data in the following table to answer questions 9–11. Assume that there are no preferred shareholders.

Parameter	Company NOP
1st quarter net income	$5,000,000
2nd quarter net income	$4,000,000
3rd quarter net income	$6,000,000
4th quarter net income	$10,000,000
Next fiscal year net income estimate	$35,000,000
Shares outstanding	$5,000,000
Market price per share	$100

9. What is the EPS of this company over the previous year?

10. What are two possible values for the P/E ratio for this company? What are the corresponding earnings yields for each?

11. What are some possible alternatives for constructing the P/E ratio with information that is not available in the previous table?

12. Which of the following are used to measure a company's cash flows?

  I. Net income before depreciation and amortization
  II. EBITDA
  III. Free cash flow less interest, other financing costs, and taxes

    a. II only

    b. I and II only

    c. II and III only

    d. I and III only

    e. I, II, and III

13. Which of the following is usually true when classifying companies by their cash flows?

    a. Mature companies have positive investment cash flows.

    b. Mature companies have positive cash flows from operations.

    c. Companies that are downsizing have positive cash flows from financing activities.

    d. Companies in financial distress have positive investment cash flows.

14. Which of the following statements is true about free cash flows?

   a. It is always good for a company to have high free cash flows.

   b. They are straightforward to calculate for real companies.

   c. All capital expenditures must be subtracted from cash flows to calculate free cash flows.

   d. They are the cash flows left over after the company funds all positive NPV projects.

15. What information does cash flow analysis provide that is more difficult to see from inspecting the balance sheet and income statement?

   a. The company's reliance on external sources to finance capital investments

   b. The company's ability to make interest payments on its debt

   c. The company's ability to convert gross profits into net profits

   d. The company's desire to grow into new markets

16. Which of the following may be a possible explanation for a declining capital expenditures coverage ratio?

   I. Recent investments are not yet generating cash.

II. The company is experiencing greater competition which is shrinking the cash flow from operations.

III. The company is becoming mature so it's not investing as much into capital expenditures.

    a. I only

    b. III only

    c. I and II only

    d. I and III only

    e. I, II, and III

17. Companies' dividend policies are usually focused on what dividend measure?

    a. Total dividends paid

    b. Dividends per share

    c. Dividend yield

    d. Dividend payout ratio

18. What are three findings of the study examining the effects of dividend yields on future dividends and stock prices?

    a. _____

    b. _____

    c. _____

19. Which of the following inputs are necessary to calculate the fair price of a stock using the constant discount rate version of the finite life general DDM?

   I. The current market price
  II. The current dividend payout ratio
 III. The discount rate

    a. II only

    b. III only

    c. I and II only

    d. II and III only

    e. I, II, and III

20. What are three shortcomings of using a dividend discount model for analyzing whether stocks are overpriced or underpriced?

    a. _____

    b. _____

    c. _____

Use this data to answer questions 21–26. Company MOP is paying a dividend of $2 a share next year. Each year after that, the dividend will grow by 5% forever. After three years, the market price will be $25. The risk-free rate is 3%, the market risk premium is 6%, and the stock's beta is 1.5.

21. Use the CAPM to calculate the appropriate discount rate for the stock of MOP.

22. Use the constant discount rate version of the finite life general DDM with a three-year horizon to calculate the fair value of MOP stock.

23. Now assume that you don't know the market price in three years. Use the constant growth DDM to calculate the fair value of MOP stock.

24. Use the constant growth DDM to calculate the fair value of stock MOP in three years. Will the stock be overpriced or underpriced in three years (i.e., will the market price be above or below its fair value at that time)?

25. Now assume that in four years the company will enter a mature phase where its dividends will grow at a slower rate. What is that new rate of growth of dividends (after four years) that will make the fair value of the stock in three years equal to its market price in three years?

26. Now assume that company MOP will instead, starting next year, either grow its dividends 5%, shrink them by 5%, or do nothing. The probability of growth is 60%, shrinking is 10%, and doing nothing is 30%. Use the tri-nomial stochastic DDM to find the fair value of the stock (let $D_0 = \$2$).

27. What are two problems that arise when using the constant growth DDM?

a. _____

b. _____

For questions 28–30, identify the following statements as *True, False,* or *Uncertain.* If *False* or *Uncertain,* explain briefly.

28. Comparing fair value to market value or comparing expected return to required return makes no difference in determining whether a stock is undervalued or overvalued.

29. One of the advantages of stochastic models is that a Monte Carlo simulation can be used to determine the probability distribution for a stock's value in the future.

30. Dividend discount models are usually good at predicting the market value of a stock.

CHAPTER 12

Security Analysis Using Value-Based Metrics

1. What is the main difference that distinguishes value-based methods of fundamental analysis from traditional methods?

   a. Interest is excluded from the calculation of a firm's profitability.

   b. Economic profitability is used instead of accounting profitability to measure a firm's performance.

   c. The CAPM is used to measure a company's cost of equity capital.

   d. After-tax profitability is used instead of pretax profitability.

Use the data in the following table to answer questions 2–10.

Parameter	Firm XYZ
Total sales	$550,000
Cost of goods sold	$380,000
Other expenses (SG&A)	$40,000
Depreciation	$30,000
Interest	$10,000
Taxes (at 40%)	$36,000
Net current assets	$80,000
Fixed assets	$220,000
Long-term debt	$100,000
Shareholder equity	$200,000

2. Calculate the firm's net profits. Is the firm generating a positive accounting profit?

3. What is the firm's basic NOPAT (excluding all special accounting adjustments)?

4. What is the firm's after-tax cost of debt (assuming that the company's bonds are trading at par and excluding all special accounting adjustments)?

5. Assume that the firm's stock has a beta of 1.5, the market risk premium is 8% and the risk-free rate is 3%. Use the CAPM model to find the firm's cost of equity.

6. What is the firm's WACC? What is its $WACC? Assume that the firm's target debt/capital ratio is 1/3.

7. Derive the firm's EVA (Economic Value Added). Is the firm generating a positive economic profit?

8. Calculate the RROC (Residual Return on Capital) of the firm.

9. Assuming that investors are willing to pay an NPV multiple of five times the estimated EVA, what is the firm's enterprise value?

10. Which of the following actions are, by themselves, likely to increase firm XYZ's EVA?

I. Using future profits to buy back long term debt
II. Adding equity into the firm by issuing shares
III. Closing offices in places that are not profitable

   a. II only

   b. III only

   c. I and III only

   d. II and III only

   e. I, II, and III

11. Which of the following changes would improve NOPAT's approximation to the firm's true after-tax operating profit?

  I. Using economic depreciation instead of accounting depreciation

  II. Adding the increase in the LIFO reserve account back into the operating profit

  III. Adding the net increase in R&D back into the operating profit

  a. I only

  b. II only

  c. I and II only

  d. II and III only

  e. I, II, and III

12. Which of the following factors is used (by Global Asset Management) in multi-factor models to model a company's expected return?

  a. Price-to-book ratio

  b. Net profit

  c. Debt-to-equity ratio

  d. NPV-to-capital ratio

13. Which of the following are differences between CFROI and EVA?

  I. CFROI is not a value-based metric.
 II. CFROI uses gross cash flow and gross capital investment measures.
III. CFROI is a dollar-based measure while EVA is not.

  a. II only

  b. III only

  c. I and III only

  d. II and III only

  e. I, II, and III

14. What does it mean that a certain company's CFROI is 10%?

  a. The company has a positive EVA and is thus a wealth creator.

  b. The company is profitable.

  c. The company's estimated after-tax IRR earned on the company's assets over 10 years is 10%.

  d. The company's estimated return on equity less taxes and interest is 10%.

For questions 15–16, identify the following statements as *True*, *False*, or *Uncertain*. If *False* or *Uncertain*, explain briefly.

15. When calculating EVA, a company's unleveraged net operating profit after tax should be used to prevent double counting of tax subsidies on interest.

16. Companies that plot above the curve in the following exhibit are undervalued by the market and offer opportunities for outperformance.

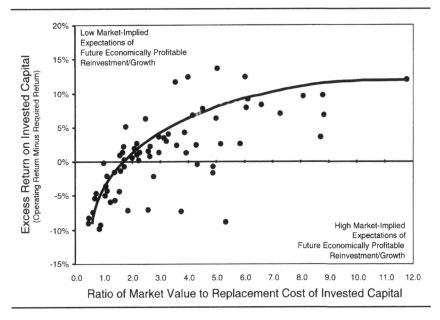

Source: James L. Grant and James A. Abate, *Focus on Value: A Corporate and Investor Guide to Wealth Creation* (New York: John Wiley & Sons, 2001).

CHAPTER 13

Multi-Factor Equity Risk Models

1. What criteria is used to choose risk factors from a set of descriptors?

2. Which of the following risk factor would likely *not* be in the volatility risk index?

   a. Daily standard deviation

   b. Historical alpha

   c. Beta times sigma

   d. Serial dependence

3. What is the major advantage of linear multi-factor risk models over traditional portfolio analysis in estimating portfolio risk?

a. The calculations are simpler.

b. Fewer inputs need to be estimated.

c. The answer is unbiased.

d. Portfolio analysis provides a very rough estimate of risk.

4. What are the three possible ways of classifying risk?

a. _____

b. _____

c. _____

Use the data in the following exhibits a. and b. to answer questions 5–7.

Analysis of Portfolio ABC's Exposures
a. Analysis of Risk Exposures to S&P 500

Factor Exposures

Risk Index Exposures (Std. Dev.)

	Mgd.	Bmk.	Act.		Mgd.	Bmk.	Act.
Volatility	0.220	−0.171	0.391	Value	−0.169	−0.034	−0.136
Momentum	0.665	−0.163	0.828	Earnings variation	0.058	−0.146	0.204
Size	−0.086	0.399	−0.485	Leverage	0.178	−0.149	0.327
Size nonlinearity	0.031	0.097	−0.067	Currency sensitivity	0.028	−0.049	0.077
Trading activity	0.552	−0.083	0.635	Yield	−0.279	0.059	−0.338
Growth	0.227	−0.167	0.395	Non-EST universe	0.032	0.000	0.032
Earnings yield	−0.051	0.081	−0.132				

Industry Weights (Percent)

	Mgd.	Bmk.	Act.		Mgd.	Bmk.	Act.
Mining & Metals	0.013	0.375	−0.362	Heavy Machinery	0.000	0.062	−0.062
Gold	0.000	0.119	−0.119	Industrial Parts	0.234	1.086	−0.852
Forestry & Paper	0.198	0.647	−0.449	Electric Utility	1.852	1.967	−0.115
Chemicals	0.439	2.386	−1.947	Gas Utilities	0.370	0.272	0.098
Energy Reserves	2.212	4.589	−2.377	Railroads	0.000	0.211	−0.211
Oil Refining	0.582	0.808	−0.226	Airlines	0.143	0.194	−0.051
Oil Services	2.996	0.592	2.404	Truck/Sea/Air Freight	0.000	0.130	−0.130
Food & Beverages	2.475	3.073	−0.597	Medical Services	1.294	0.354	0.940
Alcohol	0.000	0.467	−0.467	Medical Products	0.469	2.840	−2.370
Tobacco	0.000	0.403	−0.403	Drugs	6.547	8.039	−1.492
Home Products	0.000	1.821	−1.821	Electronic Equipment	11.052	5.192	5.860
Grocery Stores	0.000	0.407	−0.407	Semiconductors	17.622	6.058	11.564
Consumer Durables	0.165	0.125	0.039	Computer Hardware	12.057	9.417	2.640
Motor Vehicles & Parts	0.000	0.714	−0.714	Computer Software	9.374	6.766	2.608
Apparel & Textiles	0.000	0.191	−0.191	Defense & Aerospace	0.014	0.923	−0.909
Clothing Stores	0.177	0.308	−0.131	Telephone	0.907	4.635	−3.728
Specialty Retail	0.445	2.127	−1.681	Wireless Telecom.	0.000	1.277	−1.277
Department Stores	0.000	2.346	−2.346	Information Services	0.372	1.970	−1.598
Constructn. & Real Prop.	0.569	0.204	0.364	Industrial Services	0.000	0.511	−0.511
Publishing	0.014	0.508	−0.494	Life/Health Insurance	0.062	1.105	−1.044
Media	1.460	2.077	−0.617	Property/Casualty Ins.	1.069	2.187	−1.118
Hotels	0.090	0.112	−0.022	Banks	5.633	6.262	−0.630
Restaurants	0.146	0.465	−0.319	Thrifts	1.804	0.237	1.567
Entertainment	1.179	1.277	−0.098	Securities & Asst. Mgmt.	6.132	2.243	3.888
Leisure	0.000	0.247	−0.247	Financial Services	5.050	5.907	−0.857
Environmental Services	0.000	0.117	−0.117	Internet	3.348	1.729	1.618
Heavy Electrical Eqp.	1.438	1.922	−0.483	Equity REIT	0.000	0.000	0.000

Note: Mgd. = Managed; Bmk. = S&P 500 (the benchmark); Act. = Active = Managed − Benchmark

b. Analysis of Sector Exposures Relative to S&P 500

Sector Weights (Percent)

	Mgd.	Bmk.	Act.		Mgd.	Bmk.	Act.
Basic Materials	0.65	3.53	−2.88	Utility	2.22	2.24	−0.02
Mining	0.01	0.38	−0.36	Electric Utility	1.85	1.97	−0.12
Gold	0.00	0.12	−0.12	Gas Utility	0.37	0.27	0.10
Forest	0.20	0.65	−0.45	Transport	0.14	0.54	−0.39
Chemical	0.44	2.39	−1.95	Railroad	0.00	0.21	−0.21
Energy	5.79	5.99	−0.20	Airlines	0.14	0.19	−0.05
Energy Reserves	2.21	4.59	−2.38	Truck Freight	0.00	0.13	−0.13
Oil Refining	0.58	0.81	−0.23	Health Care	8.31	11.23	−2.92
Oil Services	3.00	0.59	2.40	Medical Provider	1.29	0.35	0.94
Consumer (non-cyc.)	2.48	6.17	−3.70	Medical Products	0.47	2.84	−2.37
Food/Beverage	2.48	3.07	−0.60	Drugs	6.55	8.04	−1.49
Alcohol	0.00	0.47	−0.47	Technology	53.47	30.09	23.38
Tobacco	0.00	0.40	−0.40	Electronic Equipment	11.05	5.19	5.86
Home Products	0.00	1.82	−1.82	Semiconductors	17.62	6.06	11.56
Grocery	0.00	0.41	−0.41	Computer Hardware	12.06	9.42	2.64
Consumer (cyclical)	1.36	6.01	−4.66	Computer Software	9.37	6.77	2.61
Cons. Durables	0.17	0.13	0.04	Defense & Aerospace	0.01	0.92	−0.91
Motor Vehicles	0.00	0.71	−0.71	Internet	3.35	1.73	1.62
Apparel	0.00	0.19	−0.19	Telecommunications	0.91	5.91	−5.00
Clothing	0.18	0.31	−0.13	Telephone	0.91	4.63	−3.73
Specialty Retail	0.45	2.13	−1.68	Wireless	0.00	1.28	−1.28
Dept. Store	0.00	2.35	−2.35	Commercial Services	0.37	2.48	−2.11
Construction	0.57	0.20	0.36	Information Services	0.37	1.97	−1.60
Consumer Services	2.89	4.69	−1.80	Industrial Services	0.00	0.51	−0.51
Publishing	0.01	0.51	−0.49	Financial	19.75	17.94	1.81
Media	1.46	2.08	−0.62	Life Insurance	0.06	1.11	−1.04
Hotels	0.09	0.11	−0.02	Property Insurance	1.07	2.19	−1.12
Restaurants	0.15	0.47	−0.32	Banks	5.63	6.26	−0.63
Entertainment	1.18	1.28	−0.10	Thrifts	1.80	0.24	1.57
Leisure	0.00	0.25	−0.25	Securities/Asst. Mgmt.	6.13	2.24	3.89
Industrials	1.67	3.19	−1.51	Financial Services	5.05	5.91	−0.86
Environ. Servs.	0.00	0.12	−0.12	Equity REIT	0.00	0.00	0.00
Heavy Electrical	1.44	1.92	−0.48				
Heavy Mach.	0.00	0.06	−0.06				
Industrial Parts	0.23	1.09	−0.85				

Note: Mgd = Managed; Bmk = Benchmark; Act = Active = Managed − Benchmark

5. What is the largest factor bet of Portfolio ABC relative to its benchmark?

6. What are the three largest industry bets of Portfolio ABC relative to its benchmark?

7. What are the three largest sector bets of Portfolio ABC relative to its benchmark (i.e., the 13 major sectors, not the many subsectors)?

8. Which of the following are advantages of using William Sharpe's style analysis for performance attribution?

I. It allows investors to separate the sector allocation part of the return from the stock selection part of the return.

II. It allows investors to decompose the total return into returns from various risk factors.

III. It is simple and easy to implement.

a. I only

b. III only

c. I and II only

d. I and III only

e. I, II, and III

f. None of the above

9. What are some drawbacks of using quantitative multi-factor risk models?

   I. They can not take into account important qualitative features of a security.
   II. It is nearly impossible to include all the risk factors that affect the returns of a security.
   III. Their predictive power is limited because they use past returns to represent future expected returns.

   a. I only

   b. II only

   c. I and II only

   d. II and III only

   e. I, II, and III

   f. None of the above

For questions 10–11, identify the following statements as *True*, *False*, or *Uncertain*. If *False* or *Uncertain*, explain briefly.

10. Factor models generally outperform dividend discount models in return attribution.

11. In the BARRA risk model, exposures to industry factors are measured in units of standard deviation while exposures to risk factors are measured in percentages.

Equity Derivatives I:
Features and Valuation

1. Match the following terms related to equity derivatives from Chapter 14 with their descriptions.

Terms

1. Gamma

2. Time value

3. Asian option

4. FLEX option

5. Black-Scholes model

6. Net cost of carry

7. Exotic option

8. Equity swap

9. Clearinghouse

Descriptions

a. Payout depends on the average of the spot prices over its life

b. Has more complex payoff characteristics

c. An agreement which provides for the periodic exchange of a schedule of cash flows over a period of time

d. Uses certain assumptions and arbitrage arguments to determine theoretical value of an option

e. An intermediary that takes both sides of transactions on option exchanges

f. Is traded on exchanges but allows users to customize some terms of the option contract

g. Curvature of the relationship between the value of an option and the value of the underlying

h. Adjustment of the dividend yield for the cost of financing

i. A premium paid by the option buyer in the hope that the price of the underlying will eventually move in his/her favor

2. What four roles do derivatives serve in portfolio management?

a. _____

b. _____

c. _____

d. _____

3. Which of the following are advantages of trading options on exchanges rather than on the OTC market?

I. Lower transaction costs
II. More flexibility in customizing various features
III. No counterparty risk for both buyer and seller

   a. I only

   b. III only

   c. I and III only

   d. II and III only

   e. I, II, and III

4. When can a buyer exercise an American option?

   a. At any time

   b. At any time on or before the expiration date

   c. At certain dates before the expiration date

   d. Only on the expiration date

5. What is the value of a contract of an index option when the underlying index is at 1,000?

   a. $10,000

   b. $1,000

   c. $2,000

   d. The answer can not be determined from the data given.

6. What is the major difference between LEAPS and traditional option contracts?

   a. Longer maturities

   b. Lower transaction costs

   c. Flexible strike prices

   d. Flexible contract values

For questions 7–10, identify the following statements as *True*, *False*, or *Uncertain*. If *False* or *Uncertain*, explain briefly.

7. The maximum loss on a short call position equals the strike price minus the option price.

8. The gamma of an option that is deep in the money is very close to zero.

9. The Black-Scholes formula can also be used to find the fair value of a put option.

10. A European option should be worth the same as an American option because it is pointless to exercise early and lose the option's time value.

Use this data to answer questions 11–13. An investor buys a call option for stock XYZ for $400. The option contract allows her to buy 100 shares of the stock at $100 per share at any time in the next three months. The current price of the stock is $98.

11. What is the intrinsic value of the option contract right now? What is its time value right now?

12. Assume that on the next day, the price of stock XYZ rises to $102. The price of the option per share rises from $4 to $6. What is the new intrinsic value of the contract? What is the new time value of the contract? Use this data to estimate a delta for the option.

13. At the expiration date, the price of stock XYZ is $105. What is the price per share of the option immediately before it is exercised? What is the investor's profit or loss?

14. What six factors affect the price of an American option?

a. _____

b. _____

c. _____

d. _____

e. _____

f. _____

15. Which of the following by itself would cause the price of a call option to go up?

I. The volatility of the underlying asset is expected to rise because of an imminent earnings announcement.
II. The Federal Reserve unexpectedly lowers short-term interest rates.
III. The company cuts the dividend rate in half.

a. II only

b. III only

c. I and III only

d. II and III only

e. I, II, and III

16. Which of the following is *always* preferable for a writer of a call option?

a. An option with higher delta

b. An option with higher theta

c. An option with higher vega

17. What mechanism limits the exposure to counterparty risk in futures transactions?

Use this data to answer questions 18–19. The current spot price of an index is 1,500. The annualized dividend yield of the index over a six-month period is 2%. The annualized borrowing rate for a six-month loan is 6%.

18. What is the theoretical price of a futures contract whose settlement date is six months from now?

19. Assume that the futures price in the marketplace is 1,550. Explain the step-by-step arbitrage process by which you can make a profit without risk.

20. Describe six mechanisms used in OTC derivative markets to address the issue of counterparty risk.

   a. _____

   b. _____

   c. _____

   d. _____

   e. _____

   f. _____

21. Which of the following is the major difference between first generation OTC options and second generation OTC options?

   a. The former have standardized strike prices and maturities. The latter don't.

   b. The former are usually used by institutional clients. The latter are used by retail clients.

   c. The former are also traded on exchanges. The latter are not.

   d. The former are American or European style. The latter have more complex payoff characteristics.

22. Which of the following is true about equity swaps?

   a. They are used for long-term transactions.

   b. There are usually a total of two exchanges of cash flows.

   c. They allow investors to minimize or eliminate transaction costs.

   d. They are not usually used for exchanging cash flows denominated in two different currencies.

CHAPTER 15

Equity Derivatives II: Portfolio Management Applications

1. Which of the following statements are true about protective puts?

I. They are used to hedge some or all of the underlying security's risk.
II. Their price can be likened to an insurance premium.
III. They usually lower the portfolio's expected return.

  a. I only

  b. II only

  c. I and II only

  d. II and III only

  e. I, II, and III

2. Which of the following would be the best situation to write (short) a put?

   a. An investor believes that the price of the underlying asset will double tomorrow.

   b. An investor believes that the underlying asset is over-priced and will eventually depreciate.

   c. An investor believes that the underlying asset will eventually appreciate but may be slightly overpriced in the short run.

   d. An investor believes that the underlying asset is extremely overpriced but doesn't want to sell the shares of the underlying asset and risk moving the market.

3. What are two possible reasons for creating a synthetic position in a stock instead of an actual cash position?

   a. _____

   b. _____

4. An investor would like to eventually liquidate his (or her) position in a stock, but is in no hurry and would like to earn some quick income from it. He is expecting that the price will not really move anywhere in the next three months. What is a good strategy for implementing his goals?

   a. Buy a call

   b. Write a call

c. Buy a put

d. Write a put

Use this data to answer questions 5–7. A stock portfolio has a beta of 0.5; the beta of the stock index relative to the stock index futures contract is 1.1.

5. What is the appropriate minimum risk hedge fund ratio?

a. 0.55

b. 0.5

c. 0.8

d. 1.6

6. Assume that the market value of the portfolio to be hedged is $10 million. The current value of the futures contract is 800. The multiple specified by the stock index futures contract is 100. Use this information and your answer from question 5 to calculate the number of contracts necessary to short in order to hedge the portfolio.

7. What is the appropriate hedge ratio if the manager can hedge the portfolio until the settlement date?

8. What are the disadvantages of using stock index futures and a money market instrument to create a synthetic index fund?

 I. Higher transaction costs
 II. Less control over portfolio constituents
III. Reduced returns from variation margin

   a. I only

   b. III only

   c. II and III only

   d. I and III only

   e. I, II, and III

9. What are three ways to implement enhanced indexing?

   a. _____

   b. _____

   c. _____

For questions 10–12, identify the following statements as *True*, *False*, or *Uncertain*. If *False* or *Uncertain*, explain briefly.

10. Much of what can be done with listed options and stock futures can also be done with OTC derivatives but in a more precise way.

11. The relationship between risk and return in options is consistent with the principles of the CAPM.

12. An out-of-the-money call usually has a lower beta than an in-the-money call for the same underlying asset.

13. Which of the following is true about a protective put?

    a. Its expected return is lower than the risk-free rate.

    b. Its expected return is equal to the risk-free rate.

    c. Its expected return is greater than the risk-free rate

    d. It varies.

CHAPTER 16

Fixed-Income Securities

1. Match the following terms related to fixed-income securities from Chapter 16 with their descriptions.

Terms

1. TIPS

2. Debenture bonds

3. Passthrough structure

4. Absolute priority rule

5. Sinking fund requirement

6. Coupon rate

7. Moody's

8. Junk bonds

9. Amortizing assets

10. Overcollateralization

11. Moral obligation bonds

12. Conversion ratio

Descriptions:

a. Carry a rating below the top four investment-grade categories

b. A form of internal credit used to absorb losses

c. Percentage of the par value of a bond that is paid out each year in interest

d. Treasury securities with protection from inflation

e. Entitles certificate holder to a pro rata share of the cash flow from collateral

f. Municipal bonds with a nonbinding pledge of tax revenue

g. Rating company

h. Way in which creditors are paid in the event of a bankruptcy

i. Loans in which the borrower makes scheduled principal and interest payments over the life of the loan

j. Bonds unsecured by collateral

k. Issuer must retire a portion of a bond issue each year

l. Number of shares received from exercising the call option of a convertible bond

2. What is the semiannual interest payment on a bond whose par value is $10,000 and whose coupon rate is 6%?

a. $60

b. $600

c. $300

d. $3,000

3. Which of the following statements are true concerning call provisions in a bond issue?

I. A bond with a call provision can offer a lower coupon than the same bond without a call provision.
II. A bond with refunding protection can offer a lower coupon than the same bond with call protection.
III. A bond with an earlier first call date can offer a lower coupon than the same bond with a later first call date.

a. I only

b. III only

c. I and II only

d. I, II, and III only

e. None of the above

4. Which of the following bonds with the same coupon rates, and with all else being equal, would usually trade at the highest price?

   a. A callable bond with refunding protection

   b. A noncallable bond with a put provision

   c. A callable bond with a deferred call provision

   d. A noncallable bond

5. Which of the following statements are generally true concerning Treasury bills?

   I. They pay monthly coupon interest.
  II. They are discount securities.
 III. They mature in less than one year.

   a. II only

   b. III only

   c. I and II only

   d. II and III only

   e. I, II, and III

6. How many zero-coupon strips can be issued representing single-payment claims on a 10-year U.S. Treasury Note?

   a. 21

   b. 11

   c. 10

   d. 1

7. Which of the following securities are backed by the full faith and credit of the United States federal government?

   I. Freddie Mac bonds
  II. Municipal bonds
 III. TIPS

   a. I only

   b. III only

   c. I and II only

   d. I and III only

   e. I, II, and III

For questions 8–9, identify the following statements as *True*, *False*, or *Uncertain*. If *False* or *Uncertain*, explain briefly.

8. According to the absolute priority rule, in the case of liquidation after bankruptcy, all bondholders must be reimbursed in full before stockholders can receive anything.

9. If the put option on a convertible bond is exercised by the bondholder, the issuer may choose to redeem the bond with either cash, securities, or both.

Use this data to answer questions 10–11. The par value of a convertible bond is $1,000. Its current market price is $1,200. The conversion ratio is 40, and the market price per share of the stock is $28.

10. Calculate the stated conversion price of the convertible bond.

11. Is the option to convert likely to be immediately exercised?

12. What four factors are considered in determining the credit rating of a company?

a. _____

b. _____

c. _____

d. _____

13. Which of the following statements are true about investment-grade bonds?

I. They have a low probability of default.
II. They all have a AAA (or Aaa from Moody's) rating.
III. They are as safe as U.S. Treasury securities.

a. I only

b. II only

c. III only

d. I and II only

e. I, II, and III

14. Which of the following statements are true concerning municipal bonds?

I. Their interest payments are always exempt from federal income taxes.

II. Because municipal securities are guaranteed by state income taxes, they expose investors to virtually no credit risk.

III. They may be used to fund specific projects such as stadiums, bridges, or hospitals.

a. I only

b. III only

c. I and II only

d. II and III only

e. I, II, and III

15. What are three special security structures of municipal bonds?

a. _____

b. _____

c. _____

16. Which of the following is a nonamortizing asset?

a. U.S. Treasury bond

b. Mortgage-backed securities

c. Credit card receivable-backed securities

d. Auto loan-backed securities

17. Identify five types of non-real estate-backed securities.

a. _____

b. _____

c. _____

d. _____

e. _____

18. Which of the following affect the price of an amortizing asset-backed security?

I. Projected default rate
II. Level of interest rates
III. Path of interest rates over the life of the asset

a. I only

b. I and II only

c. I and III only

d. II and III only

e. I, II, and III

19. Which of the following affect the credit rating of an ABS?

   I. Ability of the servicer to perform all the necessary servicing activities
  II. The credit rating of the senior bondholder
 III. Credit enhancements

   a. I only

   b. II only

   c. I and III only

   d. II and III only

   e. I, II, and III

   f. None of the above

20. Identify three types of external credit enhancement and three types of internal credit enhancement for asset-backed securities.

   a. _____

   b. _____

   c. _____

   d. _____

   e. _____

   f. _____

CHAPTER 17

Real Estate-Backed Securities

1. Match the following terms related to real estate-backed securities from Chapter 17 with their descriptions.

Terms

1. Refinancing burnout

2. Planned amortization class (class) CMO

3. Ginnie Mae

4. Conforming loan

5. Contraction risk

6. Balloon risk

7. Alternative A loans

8. Conditional prepayment rate (CPR)

9. Mortgage

10. Shifting interest mechanism

Descriptions

a. For borrowers who have excellent credit ratings but don't conform to some underwriting criteria of the three major agencies

b. A result of a possible drop in interest rates that forces the investor to reinvest more and more repayments at lower interest rates

c. A loan secured by collateral of real estate

d. An institution whose securities are guaranteed by the full faith and credit of the U.S. government

e. A factor affecting prepayment behavior that is related to the prior path of interest rates over the life of the pool

f. A result of the possible inability of a borrower to pay the large final principal payments, causing the lender to extend the loan

g. Method to ensure that the credit protection for the senior tranche is not eroded by prepayments

h. A mortgage that meets the underwriting standards of the three major federal agencies

i. A tranche that has priority over all other tranches in receiving principal payments from collateral, thus limiting prepayment risk

j. A convention by which the prepayment rate is assumed to be a percentage of the remaining principal in the pool

2. Which of the following are true about a fixed-rate, level-payment, fully amortized mortgage?

I. The monthly interest payments are a fixed dollar amount.

II. The monthly principal payments are a fixed percentage of the outstanding principal.

III. If there are no prepayments, the outstanding principal balance decreases linearly until the maturity date.

a. I only

b. III only

c. I and II only

d. I and III only

e. I, II, and III

f. None of the above

3. Which of the following mortgage candidates would be *most* likely to be approved, all else being equal?

a. PTI = 30%, LTV = 50%

b. PTI = 60%, LTV = 110%

c. PTI = 30%, LTV = 110%

d. PTI = 60%, LTV = 50%

Use this data to answer questions 4–5. The monthly payment on a $200,000 fixed-rate, level-payment, fully amortized mortgage of a certain maturity is determined to be $1,193. The annual mortgage rate is 6%.

4. What is the interest portion (in dollars) of the first monthly payment? What is the principal portion (in dollars) of the first monthly payment?

5. Assuming that there were no prepayments, what are the interest and principal portions (in dollars) of the last monthly payment?

6. Which of the following are always true concerning an agency/conventional mortgage passthrough?

I. It is guaranteed by the full faith and credit of the U.S. government.
II. All mortgages included in the collateral pool are conforming loans.
III. All mortgages included in the collateral pool have the same maturity.

a. II only

b. III only

c. I and II only

d. II and III only

e. I, II, and III

f. None of the above

7. Which of the following are true about the payments to the securityholders of a mortgage passthrough security?

I. Payments are made monthly.
II. Total payments to securityholders are less than the total monthly cash flows from the underlying mortgages.
III. Each securityholder receives a fraction of the total payment determined by the number of certificates he or she is holding.

a. I only

b. II only

c. I and II only

d. II and III only

e. I, II, and III

Use this data to answer questions 8–12. An investor owns shares in a $500 million passthrough with a 9% passthrough rate, a WAC of 9.75%, and a WAM of 336 months, and which is 120 PSA.

8. Calculate the first coupon payment. How much of this coupon passes through to the certificate holders? How much is used for servicing fees?

9. What is the conditional payment rate (CPR) in the first month? (Hint: The mortgage is seasoned 24 months.)

10. What is the single monthly mortality rate (SMM) in the first month?

11. Assuming that the scheduled principal payment in the first month is $336,290, how much principal will likely be prepaid in the first month?

12. The investor holds 12 (out of a total of 10,000) certificates in this mortgage passthrough. What will be his payment in the first month?

13. During which of the following times is there a drop in pre-payments?

    a. Falling interest rates

    b. Summer

    c. Strong economic growth

    d. None of the above

14. What are the two main reasons that a homeowner would prepay a mortgage?

    a. _____

    b. _____

For questions 15–18, identify the following statements as *True*, *False*, or *Uncertain*. If *False* or *Uncertain*, explain briefly.

15. A prepaid penalty mortgage is likely to have a lower price (or equivalently, a higher coupon rate) than a comparable mortgage without a penalty.

16. The WAM is defined as the sum of the principal payments from a mortgage passthrough weighted by the time when they are paid.

17. A drop in interest rates from 12% to 10% would cause prepayments to rise significantly.

18. An investor concerned with contraction risk can instead buy principal-only securities to eliminate this risk.

19. Which of the following is a *positive* effect of lower interest rates on interest-only securities?

    a. More prepayments

    b. Less prepayments

    c. Higher rate of discounting

    d. Lower rate of discounting

20. What are three types of agency collaterized mortgage obligations (CMOs)?

    a. _____

    b. _____

    c. _____

21. Which of the following tranches provides the best protection against contraction risk?

    a. The A tranche in a sequential-pay CMO structure

    b. The D tranche in a sequential-pay CMO structure

    c. The Z (accrual) tranche in a sequential-pay CMO structure

    d. The support tranche in a PAC CMO structure

22. Which of the following might cause a borrower to seek a nonagency loan?

  I. The borrower is a small-business owner who can't provide adequate income verification documents.

 II. The borrower has already defaulted on a loan in the past and has a bad credit history.

III. The borrower wants to take out a very large loan.

    a. I only

    b. I and II only

    c. II and III only

    d. I and III only

    e. I, II, and III

23. Which of the following is true of the default rate of a 150 SDA mortgage pool?

I. The annual default rate in the first month is 0.03%.

II. The annual default rate in the 35th month is 0.90%.

III. The annual default rate in the 123rd month is 0.045%.

   a. I only

   b. II only

   c. I and II only

   d. I and III only

   e. I, II, and III

24. What are two additional credit enhancements available for nonagency mortgage-backed securities?

   a. _____

   b. _____

25. What are four forms of call protection for investors in commercial mortgage-backed securities?

   a. _____

   b. _____

   c. _____

   d. _____

For questions 26–27, identify the following statements as *True*, *False*, or *Uncertain*. If *False* or *Uncertain*, explain briefly.

26. For nonagency mortgage-backed securities, the PPC benchmark is issuer specific.

27. An NAS tranche reduces both contraction risk and extension risk.

CHAPTER 18

General Principles of Bond Valuation

1. What are the three steps to finding the present value of a financial asset?

   a. _____

   b. _____

   c. _____

2. Which of the following differences (all else being equal) would cause two securities, A and B, to have different present values?

   I. A is a callable bond; B is not a callable bond
   II. A is a Treasury bond; B is a corporate bond
   III. A is a more liquid bond; B is a less liquid bond

   a. II only

   b. I and II only

c. I and III only

d. II and III only

e. I, II, and III

3. Which of the following is *not* true about U.S. Treasury bonds?

    a. Their interest rates are used as the benchmark interest rates.

    b. They are always issued as coupon-paying securities.

    c. They are some of the easiest real-world bonds to price.

    d. They have no (or negligible) default risk.

4. What are the three basic factors that determine the appropriate discount rate for a particular security's cash flows?

    a. _____

    b. _____

    c. _____

Use this data to answer questions 5–9. Assume that the theoretical spot rate curve is flat at 9%.

5. What is the price (i.e., present value) of a 5-year, 10% coupon bond with a par value of $100? Why is it trading at a premium?

6. Now assume that the spot rate curve is flat at 10% (not 9%). What is the price (i.e., present value) of a 5-year, 10% coupon bond with a par value of $100?

7. Now assume that you bought the same 5-year, 10% coupon bond with a par value of $100, 109 days after it was issued. The current coupon period has 183 days. The theoretical spot rate curve is again flat at 9%. What is the full price of the bond?

8. How much interest accrued over the 109 days? What is the clean price of the bond in question 7?

9. What two factors account for the decrease in the price of the bond from $103.96 to $103.74 over 109 days, even though interest rates remained unchanged at 9%?

a. _____

b. _____

10. Which of the following statements are true about the price/discount rate relationship between a bond?

I. When the discount rate exceeds the coupon rate, the bond trades at a discount.

II. Price and discount rate have an inverse linear relationship.

III. When interest rates rise, bond prices increase but at a decreasing rate.

a. I only

b. III only

c. I and II only

d. I and III only

e. I, II, and III

Use the data in the following table to answer questions 11–13.

Years to Maturity	Annual Yield to Maturity
6-month T-bill	2.4%
1.0-Year T-bill	2.9%
1.5-Year T-note	3.3%
2.0-Year T-note	3.5%

Both T-bills are traded as discount securities (no coupons). Both T-notes are trading at par value and make semiannual coupon payments until maturity.

11. What is the price of the 6-month T-bill? What is the price of the 1-year T-bill?

12. Use the bootstrapping method to calculate the theoretical spot rate (annual) on a zero-coupon 1.5-year Treasury security.

13. Use the bootstrapping method and the answer to question 12 to calculate the theoretical spot rate (annual) on a zero-coupon 2-year Treasury security.

14. Which of the following strategies would lead to an arbitrage profit if strips are trading at the yield to maturity of a Treasury bond (of the same maturity as the strip) instead of the theoretical spot rate? (Assume that the par yield curve is upward sloping.)

    a. Sell short Treasury bonds—Buy the strips

    b. Sell short strips—Buy Treasury bonds

    c. Sell strips—Buy corporate bonds

    d. Sell short corporate bonds—Buy strips

For questions 15–16, identify the following statements as *True*, *False*, or *Uncertain*. If *False* or *Uncertain*, explain briefly.

15. Because strips are in every way identical to zero-coupon Treasuries, strip rates can be used as the theoretical spot rates.

16. The cash flows of non-Treasury securities are discounted at the Treasury spot rates plus a spread to account for additional risks.

CHAPTER 19

Yield Measures and Forward Rates

1. What are the three components of the dollar return from a fixed-income security?

   a. _____

   b. _____

   c. _____

2. If the bond is noncallable and is held till maturity, which of the three components in question 1 are *not* known in advance?

Use this data to answer questions 3–8. A 3-year, 8%-coupon Treasury note is trading at a discount price of $98.25. It was issued yesterday so the accrued income can be assumed to be negligible. Assume that all coupons can be reinvested at the 4% semiannual interest rate.

3. What is the total dollar return on this bond if it is purchased at the market price and held to maturity?

4. Decompose the total dollar return into the three components from question 1.

5. What is the current yield of this bond?

6. Use trial and error (or a spreadsheet program) to calculate the bond-equivalent yield to maturity of this bond. Is it higher than the current yield? Why or why not?

7. If the investors were able to realize the yield to maturity, what would be the bond's total dollar return?

8. Why is the answer in question 7 different from the answer in question 3?

9. Which of the following bonds has the lowest exposure to reinvestment risk?

   a. 10-year, 5% coupon bond with a yield to maturity of 6%

   b. 10-year, 7% coupon bond with a yield to maturity of 6%

   c. 5-year, 5% coupon bond with a yield to maturity of 6%

   d. 5-year, 7% coupon bond with a yield to maturity of 6%

For questions 10–12, identify the following statements as *True*, *False*, or *Uncertain*. If *False* or *Uncertain*, explain briefly.

10. The portfolio yield is just the average of the yields of each of the constituents weighted by their market value.

11. The steeper the term structure, the larger the divergence between the Z-spread and the nominal spread of a bond.

12. Forward rates represent the market's expectation of future interest rates.

13. Which of the following is the *best* explanation of why the Z-spread is superior to the nominal spread?

   a. It is much easier to calculate.

   b. It better reflects the credit and liquidity risk of a non-Treasury bond.

   c. It can be calculated relative to any benchmark.

   d. It accounts for the full term structure of both the bond and the benchmark.

Use this data to answer questions 14–15. The 5-year Treasury spot rate is 5%, while the 15-year Treasury spot rate is 5.34%.

14. What is the implicit forward rate on a theoretical 10-year zero-coupon Treasury note issued five years from now?

15. Assume that you could borrow and lend without risk at the Treasury spot rate. Also assume that you can now enter into a forward contract to borrow or lend without risk at a 5.6% annual rate starting in five years and ending in 15 years. Outline the steps to making a risk-free profit. What is the arbitrage profit in annual basis points?

16. Which of the following statements are true?

I. An upward-sloping spot curve necessarily means that implied short-term forwards are higher than the current short-term spot rate.

II. An upward-sloping spot curve necessarily means that the market is expecting interest rates to rise.

III. An upward sloping spot curve necessarily means that interest rates will rise.

a. I only

b. II only

c. I and II only

d. I and III only

e. I, II, and III only

CHAPTER 20

Valuation of Bonds with Embedded Options

1. Which of the following is true about the component transactions in a callable bond?

   a. The issuer is long an option-free bond; the investor is long a call option on that bond.

   b. The issuer is short an option-free bond; the investor is long a call option on that bond.

   c. The issuer is long an option-free bond; the investor is short a call option on that bond.

   d. The issuer is short an option-free bond; the investor is short a call option on that bond.

2. Which of the following is true about the component transactions in a putable bond?

a. The issuer is long an option-free bond; the investor is
long a put option on that bond.

b. The issuer is short an option-free bond; the investor is
long a put option on that bond.

c. The issuer is long an option-free bond; the investor is
short a put option on that bond.

d. The issuer is short an option-free bond; the investor is
short a put option on that bond.

3. Which of the following statements are true concerning the
option-adjusted spread, but false concerning the zero-volatility spread?

I. It is a spread over a benchmark curve or series of curves.
II. It assumes that volatility is constant.
III. It equals zero for an option-free bond.

a. I only

b. II only

c. I and II only

d. II and III only

e. I, II, and III

f. None of the above

4. Which of the following are usually true?

I. For putable bonds, zero-volatility spread exceeds option-adjusted spread.
II. For callable bonds, the option cost is positive.
III. For putable bonds, the option cost is negative.

a. II only

b. III only

c. I and III only

d. II and III only

e. I, II, and III

f. None of the above

5. The standard deviation of the 1-year rate is known to be 65 basis points. The current one-year spot rate is 5.0%. What is the value of the volatility parameter σ?

a. 7.7%

b. 6.5%

c. 13%

d. 5.65%

The following table depicts a binomial tree where all interest rates are one-year rates. At any node in the tree, there is a 50% chance that the next year's node will be right above it, and a 50% chance that the next year's node will be right below it. The interest rates are based on an interest rate model and a certain volatility parameter, σ.

Use the data in this tree to answer questions 6 to 10.

Today	Year 1	Year 2	Year 3	Year 4
				$r_{4HHHH} = 7.805\%$
			$r_{3HHH} = 7.715\%$	
		$r_{2HH} = 6.705\%$		$r_{4HHHL} = 7.062\%$
	$r_{1H} = 5.642\%$		$r_{3HHL} = 6.981\%$	
$r_0 = 4.6\%$		$r_{2HL} = 6.067\%$		$r_{4HHLL} = 6.390\%$
	$r_{1L} = 5.105\%$		$r_{3HLL} = 6.317\%$	
		$r_{2LL} = 5.490\%$		$r_{4HLLL} = 5.782\%$
			$r_{3LLL} = 5.716\%$	
				$r_{4LLLL} = 5.232\%$

6. What is the assumed volatility parameter (σ) of the one-year rate in this tree?

7. Assuming that the interest rate model and volatility assumptions are all correct, what is the theoretical value of a 5-year, 5% coupon bond, with a par value of $100? Draw a tree of the future theoretical prices of the bond (the 5% coupons are paid annually).

8. Now assume that the bond from question 7 is putable in (or after) two years at a price of $98. What is the value of the putable bond? (The bondholder will choose to sell the issue if it is trading below the put price.)

9. What is the value of the put option in question 8?

10. What is a possible value of the put option if the volatility of interest rates was doubled?

I. $0
II. $1
III. $2

a. II only

b. III only

c. I and II only

d. II and III only

e. I, II, and III

11. What is true about the option-adjusted spread of a callable bond of a corporation if the benchmark rates are on-the-run Treasuries?

I. It is usually positive.
II. It includes compensation for the option risk.
III. It includes compensation for firm-specific credit and liquidity risk.

a. I only

b. III only

c. I and II only

d. I and III only

e. I, II, and III

f. None of the above

12. What is true about the option-adjusted spread of a callable bond of a corporation if the benchmark rates are the on-the-run rates for a corporation of similar credit rating?

I. It is usually positive.
II. It includes compensation for the option risk.
III. It includes compensation for firm-specific credit and liquidity risk.

a. I only

b. III only

c. I and II only

d. I and III only

e. I, II, and III

f. None of the above

13. Which of the following are necessary inputs into a Monte Carlo simulation to calculate the option-adjusted spread of a mortgage-backed security?

   I. Today's term structure of interest rates
  II. Factors that affect the prepayment rate
 III. Volatility assumption

   a. I only

   b. II only

   c. I and II only

   d. II and III only

   e. I, II, and III

For questions 14–16, identify the following statements as *True*, *False*, or *Uncertain*. If *False* or *Uncertain*, explain briefly.

14. The Z-spread is a useful measure for asset-backed securities that either don't have a prepayment option or asset-backed securities where borrowers don't usually prepay even when refinancing rates fall below the loan rate.

15. The simulated paths of 1-month future interest rates in a Monte Carlo simulation for a mortgage-backed security are only necessary to properly discount cash flows to the present because the cash flows are known in advance.

16. CMO support tranches are usually offered at a lower nominal spread than CMO senior tranches.

CHAPTER 21

Measuring Interest Rate Risk

1. What four characteristics of a bond affect its price volatility?

   a. _____

   b. _____

   c. _____

   d. _____

2. Which of the following bonds is likely to have the highest price sensitivity to a change in yield?

   a. High coupon—Long maturity

   b. Zero coupon—Long maturity

   c. High coupon—Short maturity

   d. Zero coupon—Short maturity

3. Which of the following are implied by the convex relationship between yield and price of option-free bonds?

  I. For bondholders, the capital gain from a decrease in yield is greater than the capital loss from an increase in yield of the same magnitude.

 II. Using duration to approximate the change in price from a yield shock will always underestimate the true price.

III. The bond price will not equal zero even if interest rates rise to astronomical levels.

  a. I only

  b. III only

  c. I and II only

  d. II and III only

  e. I, II, and III

  f. None of the above

4. Which of the following is true about putable bonds?

  a. They have a region of negative convexity at low yields.

  b. They have a region of negative convexity at high yields.

  c. They exhibit price compression at low yields.

  d. They exhibit price compression at high yields.

5. What is true of a mortgage whose embedded option is out-of-the-money?

I. It is very likely to be prepaid.
II. Current interest rates are higher than the loan rate.
III. Its value is in a region of negative convexity.

   a. II only

   b. III only

   c. I and III only

   d. II and III only

   e. I, II, and III

Use the data in the following table to answer questions 6–10, and 20–22.

Price of a 5%-Coupon, 10-Year T-Note	Yield to Maturity
$108.176	4%
$101.574	4.8%
$100	5%
$98.456	5.2%
$92.561	6%

6. If its current yield to maturity is 5%, calculate the bond's duration using a rate shock of 20 basis points.

7. Repeat the calculation in question 6 using a rate shock of 100 basis points.

8. Is there a significant difference between the two calculations? Why or why not? Would your answer change if the bond had an embedded option?

9. Use your answer from question 6 to calculate the approximate price of the bond if the yield to maturity rises to 7%.

10. Is the true price likely to be higher or lower than what was calculated in question 9?

Use this data to answer questions 11–13. A 2-year, zero-coupon, option-free bond is trading at a discount price of $94.26 and has a maturity value of $100.

11. What is the Macaulay duration of the bond?

12. What is the modified duration of the bond?

13. What is always true of the Macaulay duration of a zero-coupon option-free bond?

Use this data to answer questions 14–16. A certain portfolio contains one bond with market value of $50,000 and a duration of 6 and another bond with market value of $40,000 and a duration of 8.

14. What is the duration of the portfolio?

15. What is the contribution of the first bond to the portfolio's duration?

16. Suppose the investor wants to lower the interest rate risk of the portfolio by lowering the duration to 5. Suggest a way that this can be accomplished without changing the market value of the portfolio.

Use the data in the following table to answer questions 17–19.

Key Rates	Durations of Bond A	Durations of Bond B
1-year	0.5	1.2
5-year	0.8	3.2
10-year	3.9	2.3
30-year	4.5	1.6
Duration	9	9

17. Which of the two bonds has more exposure to a parallel movement in the yield curve?

18. If the economy is expected to accelerate (but the Federal Reserve hasn't yet moved up short-term interest rates), what is the likely slope of the yield curve? Which of these bonds is likely to suffer a larger decline?

19. Which of the following is *not* a good candidate for being Bond A or Bond B?

    a. 30-year coupon-bearing Treasury bond

    b. 15-year zero-coupon bond

    c. 5-year zero-coupon bond

For questions 20–23, use the information from the table used for questions 5–10.

20. Using a rate shock of 20 basis points, calculate the convexity of the 5% coupon, 10-year, Treasury note. (Use the version of the formula with a 2 in the denominator).

21. Repeat the approximation in question 9, but adjust for convexity to get a better approximation.

22. For option-free bonds, what is the direction of the convexity adjustment? Why?

23. Use the duration and convexity of the bond to estimate its price value of a basis point (PVBP).

For questions 24–25, identify the following statements as *True*, *False*, or *Uncertain*. If *False* or *Uncertain*, explain briefly.

24. The term spread duration is ambiguous because there are three types of spreads that can change.

25. All bonds with the same duration have the same interest rate risk.

CHAPTER 22

Fixed-Income Portfolio Strategies

1. Investors in fixed-income securities are exposed to what six types of risk?

   a. _____

   b. _____

   c. _____

   d. _____

   e. _____

   f. _____

2. Of the six types of risk in question 1, how many are *substantial* risks faced by U.S. investors investing in U.S. Treasury securities?

a. 1—Interest rate risk

b. 2—Interest rate risk and yield curve risk

c. 4—Interest rate risk, yield curve risk, liquidity risk, and call risk

d. 5—Interest rate risk, yield curve risk, credit risk, liquidity risk, exchange rate risk

3. Of the six types of risk in question 1, how many are *substantial* risks faced by U.S. investors investing in French AAA corporate callable bonds?

a. 2—Yield curve risk and exchange rate risk

b. 3—Interest rate risk, yield curve risk, and call risk

c. 4—Interest rate risk, yield curve risk, call risk, and liquidity risk

d. 6—Interest rate risk, yield curve risk, call risk, credit risk, liquidity risk, and exchange rate risk

4. What are three types of credit risk?

a. _____

b. _____

c. _____

5. Which of the following is *least* concerned with liquidity risk?

   a. A bond mutual fund that invests mostly in U.S. Treasuries

   b. An institutional investor who is holding some junk and corporate issues, and trades often

   c. An individual investor who is holding long-term corporate issues for only one year when they will need to be sold for retirement income

   d. An employee whose yearly bonus is paid in 3-month T-bills

Use this data to answer questions 6–7. An investor has a 2-year investment horizon. Semiannual coupons are expected to be reinvested at the coupon rate minus 20 basis points.

6. What is the potential total return (over the investment horizon) of an on-the-run, 10-year, 5% coupon, U.S. Treasury-note whose market price is $100 and whose horizon price is $103? Express your answer in both a bond-equivalent basis and an effective rate basis.

7. Which of the two answers to question 6 is the appropriate one to use when comparing to a bond benchmark index? Why?

8. Which of the following inputs are required to perform a total return calculation?

I. Investment horizon
II. Purchase price
III. Coupon reinvestment rate

    a. I only

    b. III only

    c. I and II only

    d. I and III only

    e. I, II, and III

9. What are two possible approaches for analyzing total returns for multiple scenarios?

   a. _____

   b. _____

10. Which of the following are true about a pure bond indexing strategy?

   I. It is an optimal strategy when trying to satisfy a predetermined liability.
   II. It is more difficult to construct an indexed portfolio when the portfolio constituents are illiquid.
   III. Duration of the portfolio should equal the duration of the index.

   a. I only

   b. II only

   c. I and II only

   d. II and III only

   e. I, II, and III

11. What is the *main* difference between the enhanced index-
    ing and pure indexing approaches?

    a. Enhanced indexing allows the duration of the portfolio
       to differ from the duration of the index.

    b. Enhanced indexing makes it easier to outperform market
       returns.

    c. Enhanced indexing allows the portfolio manager not to
       buy every security in the index.

    d. Enhanced indexing charges lower fees.

12. What are appropriate active strategies if a portfolio man-
    ager believes that the economy will improve in 6 to 12
    months?

   I. Betting on the yield curve to slope upward
  II. Betting on spreads between Treasuries and corporate secu-
      rities to narrow
 III. Betting on spreads between callable and noncallable bonds
      to narrow

    a. I only

    b. I and II only

    c. I and III only

    d. II and III only

    e. I, II, and III

13. What is true of the duration of a leveraged portfolio?

   a. It is greater than the duration of the same unleveraged portfolio.

   b. It is equal to the duration of the same unleveraged portfolio.

   c. It is less than the duration of the same unleveraged portfolio.

   d. The relationship varies.

14. What is the main advantage of the repo market for collaterized borrowing?

   a. Less credit risk

   b. Lower borrowing rates

   c. Higher liquidity

   d. Lower transaction costs

15. The G.A.T. performance attribution model decomposes a portfolio's return into which five parts? Describe each.

   a. _____

   b. _____

   c. _____

   d. _____

   e. _____

16. What is true of an effectively immunized portfolio?

  I. It should be rebalanced on a weekly basis to ensure that the duration doesn't wander off from the target duration.
  II. It is easier to keep it effectively immunized if the constituents are liquid.
  III. The duration should equal the portfolio's time horizon.

  a. I only

  b. III only

  c. I and II only

  d. II and III only

  e. I, II, and III

17. What is immunization risk?

  a. The risk that there will be nonparallel shifts in the yield curve

  b. The risk that the duration of the portfolio exceeds the proper duration

  c. The risk that the duration of the portfolio is too low

  d. The risk that the cash flows of the liabilities are not met by the immunized portfolio

For questions 18–19, identify the following statements as *True*, *False*, or *Uncertain*. If *False* or *Uncertain*, explain briefly.

18. Leveraging allows a manager to increase the returns from any superior information on future interest rates.

19. Cash flow matching is a method to meet multiple future liabilities.

CHAPTER 23

Bond Portfolio Analysis Relative to a Benchmark

Use the data in the following table to answer questions 1–3.

Invest-Rite Portfolio versus Gov/Credit Index:
Market Structure Report, October 31, 1999

Duration Range		% of Market Value			Adjusted Duration			Contrib. to Duration		
		Govt.	Corp.	Total	Govt.	Corp.	Total	Govt.	Corp.	Total
0–3	Portfolio	0.8	0.0	0.8	2.71	0.00	2.71	0.02	0.00	0.02
	Index	26.4	7.1	33.5	1.80	2.06	1.85	0.47	0.15	0.62
	Diff.	−25.6	−7.1	−32.7	0.92	−2.06	0.86	−0.45	−0.15	−0.60
3–7	Portfolio	46.2	49.7	95.8	5.00	5.20	5.10	2.31	2.59	4.89
	Index	21.4	16.6	38.0	4.59	5.05	4.79	0.98	0.84	1.82
	Diff.	24.7	33.1	57.8	0.41	0.16	0.31	1.32	1.75	3.07
7–10	Portfolio	3.1	0.2	3.3	7.02	7.02	7.02	0.22	0.02	0.23
	Index	6.5	4.7	11.2	8.68	8.42	8.57	0.56	0.40	0.96
	Diff.	−3.4	−4.5	−7.9	−1.67	−1.39	−1.55	−0.34	−0.38	−0.72
10+	Portfolio	0.0	0.0	0.0	0.00	0.00	0.00	0.00	0.00	0.00
	Index	12.4	4.9	17.3	11.64	11.26	11.53	1.44	0.55	2.00
	Diff.	−12.4	−4.9	−17.3	−11.64	−11.26	−11.53	−1.44	−0.55	−2.00
Total	Portfolio	50.1	49.9	100.0	5.08	5.21	5.15	2.55	2.60	5.15
	Index	66.7	33.3	100.0	5.19	5.80	5.40	3.46	1.93	5.40
	Diff.	−16.6	16.6	0.0	−0.11	−0.59	−0.25	−0.92	0.67	−0.25

1. Compare the exposure of the portfolio to corporate securities relative to the benchmark. Which one is more sensitive to movement in corporate bonds? Why?

2. Compare the exposure of the portfolio to different length maturities relative to the benchmark.

3. Is this portfolio likely to be actively managed or passively managed?

4. Which of the following is a disadvantage of cell-based comparison analysis?

I. It doesn't quantify the magnitude of any mismatches.
II. It is difficult to identify whether any mismatches will lead to return deviations.
III. It ignores the correlation between different risk factors.

a. I only

b. II only

c. I and II only

d. II and III only

e. I, II, and III

5. What are the two main approaches for constructing index proxy portfolios?

   a. _____

   b. _____

6. What is "portable alpha"?

   a. The difference between using futures (or swaps) and cash to track a benchmark

   b. A portfolio strategy for transferring excess performance from areas of expertise to a particular benchmark

   c. A Greek letter of the alphabet

   d. Both A and B

CHAPTER 24

Multi-Factor Fixed-Income Risk Models and Their Applications

1. Which of the following are some of the uses of a multi-factor risk model?

I. Determining the risk profile of a portfolio
II. Describing the contribution of various mismatches to the total tracking error
III. Deciding which securities should be chosen for superior tracking or a benchmark index

  a. I only

  b. II only

  c. I and II only

  d. II and III only

  e. I, II, and III

2. Which of the following is the most important use of a risk model for passive managers?

   a. Determing the risk profile of the portfolio

   b. Describing the contribution of various mismatches to the total tracking error

   c. Deciding which securities should be chosen for superior tracking or a benchmark index

   d. Finding the correlations among the different risk factors

3. What are the two main outputs from applying a risk model to a portfolio?

   a. _____

   b. _____

4. Which of the following is *not* considered a systematic risk factor?

   a. Term structure risk

   b. Concentration risk

   c. Sector risk

   d. Credit quality risk

For questions 5–7, identify the following statements as *True*, *False*, or *Uncertain*. If *False* or *Uncertain*, explain briefly.

5. If there are large cash flow mismatches for certain maturities, it will always translate into a large tracking error.

6. The sum of the tracking errors from systematic and non-systematic risk sources equals the total tracking error of the portfolio.

7. The units used for risk factors and factor loadings are different for different sources of risk.

Use the data in the following table to answer questions 8–10.

	Estimated Specific Risk Volatility	% of Portfolio	% of Benchmark
Bond A	73 basis points	1.63%	0.04%
Bond B	23 basis points	9.25%	0.09%

8. Calculate the contribution to annualized tracking error of Bond A.

9. Calculate the contribution to annualized tracking error of Bond B.

10. What are two ways to minimize a portfolio's tracking error from nonsystematic risk sources?

   a. _____

   b. _____

11. Which of the following is *not* true concerning the calculation of tracking error?

    a. The order in which additional risk factors are added is
important in determining their contribution to the cumulative tracking error.

    b. The cumulative tracking error after all the systematic
risk factors are included is just the total systematic tracking error.

    c. The correlations among risk factors are not necessary for
calculating the contribution of the first term to cumulative tracking error.

    d. The sum of the isolated tracking errors of all the systematic
risk components equals the total systematic tracking error.

12. Which of the following statements concerning sigma is *not*
true?

    a. The difference between the sigma of a portfolio and the
sigma of a benchmark is equivalent to the portfolio's
tracking error.

    b. Nonsystematic components of portfolio risk contribute
very little to the sigma of a portfolio.

    c. Sigma represents the absolute return volatility of a portfo-
lio, and is not based on differences from the benchmark.

    d. The reduction of tracking error will typically bring the
portfolio sigma nearer to the sigma of the benchmark.

13. Identify three applications of risk models to portfolio management.

   a. _____

   b. _____

   c. _____

For questions 14–15, identify the following statements as *True*, *False*, or *Uncertain*. If *False* or *Uncertain*, explain briefly.

14. Risk model optimization is only used by passive managers who need to minimize portfolio tracking error.

15. A portfolio with a high sigma is more risky than a portfolio with a low sigma.

CHAPTER 25

Fixed-Income Derivatives and Risk Control

1. Identify whether each of the following characteristics belong to futures, forwards, or both (assuming that the forwards are not marked to market):

   a. Exposure to substantial counterparty risk

   b. Traded on exchanges

   c. No immediate exchange of cash

   d. Not standardized

   e. Margin is required

2. Which of the following statements are true of Treasury bond futures?

I. They are marked to market on a daily basis.

II. It is possible for a seller of a contract to avoid having to deliver a bond by buying the same contract to offset the short position.

III. Since the product to be delivered is a hypothetical 20-year coupon bond, the investor needs to settle the contract with cash.

a. I only

b. III only

c. I and II only

d. I and III only

e. I, II, and III

Use this data to answer questions 3–6. An investor purchases a 60-day futures contract whose settlement price is 102-16 (102½) and whose underlying is a U.S. Treasury bond with $100,000 in par value. The conversion factor for the cheapest-to-deliver issue is 0.9102. Assume there is no accrued interest or interim payments over the life of the futures contract.

3. What will be the invoice price?

4. What is the 60-day (nonannualized) implied repo rate if the cheapest-to-deliver issue has a market price of $92-20 (92.625) at the time that the contract is purchased?

5. Now assume that there is another issue that can be delivered whose market price is $93-31 ($93.96875) and whose conversion factor is 0.9263. Calculate the invoice price for the delivery of this issue. What is the 60-day (nonannualized) implied repo rate?

6. Based on the implied repo rates calculated in questions 4 and 5, which of the two should be delivered?

7. Which of the following transactions would be appropriate for someone who wants to lend at the implied repo rate using the futures market?

 a. Buy Treasuries—Buy futures

 b. Buy Treasuries—Sell futures

 c. Sell Treasuries—Buy futures

 d. Sell Treasuries—Sell futures

8. Which of the following are options of the long position in a futures contract?

 I. Quality option
 II. Timing option
 III. Wild card option

 a. I only

 b. II only

 c. I and II only

 d. II and III only

 e. I, II, and III

 f. None of the above

9. A change in which of the following variables would affect the value of a Treasury bond futures contract?

   a. Reinvestment rate on interim cash flows

   b. Price of the cheapest-to-deliver issue

   c. Value of delivery options of the long position

   d. All of the above

10. What are three reasons for the deviation of an actual futures prices from its theoretical value under the cost of carry model?

   a. _____

   b. _____

   c. _____

11. Which of the following are true of Eurodollar CD futures contracts?

   I. Their underlying asssets are denominated in a foreign currency (i.e., not U.S. dollars).
   II. At settlement, the short position must deliver the CD to the long position.
   III. They are used to lock in a 3-month lending or borrowing rate at a future time.

a. II only

b. III only

c. I and II only

d. II and III only

e. I, II, and III

f. None of the above

12. What are three advantages of using interest rate futures instead of long-term Treasuries to speculate on the direction of interest rates?

a. _____

b. _____

c. _____

Use this data to answer questions 13–15. A portfolio manager is instructed by clients to have the duration of their $150 million portfolio *not* exceed the target value of 4. The portfolio currently has a dollar duration of $9 million for a 100 basis point change in interest rates.

13. What is the duration of the portfolio? Does the portfolio meet the clients' specifications?

14. How can futures be used to meet the clients' targets?

15. If the dollar duration (from a 100 basis point change in rates) of the cheapest-to-deliver issue is $4,200, and the conversion factor for the cheapest-to-deliver issue is 1.04, how many futures contracts must be bought or sold to meet the client's targets?

For questions 16–17, identify the following statements as *True*, *False*, or *Uncertain*. If *False* or *Uncertain*, explain briefly.

16. An incorrect valuation model can make hedging bonds with futures an extremely risky venture.

17. The floating-rate payer in an interest rate swap does not have exposure to interest rate changes.

18. Which of the following is true of the risk-return characteristics of a fixed-rate payer in an interest rate swap?

   a. The fixed-rate payer is effectively long a package of forward contracts on a certain interest rate.

   b. The fixed-rate payer would profit from lower interest rates.

   c. The fixed-rate payer has a portfolio with positive duration.

   d. The fixed-rate payer does not face any interest rate risk because payments are fixed.

19. What is the dollar duration of a swap for a floating-rate payer if the dollar duration of a fixed-rate bond is $70 million?

    a. $7 million

    b. –$70 million

    c. $70 million

    d. Largely depends on the dollar duration of the floating-rate bond

20. What are three assumptions of the Black-Scholes option pricing model that make it inappropriate for pricing interest rate options? What is the appropriate method?

    a. _____

    b. _____

    c. _____

    d. _____

21. Suppose that an investor buys an interest rate cap for which the reference rate is 3-month LIBOR, the strike rate is 4%, settlement occurs every three months, and the notional principal is $5 million. What is the first payment if the 3-month LIBOR rises to 5%?

22. Suppose the situation is the same as in question 21 except the investor bought an interest rate floor. What is the first payment?

23. What are three methods of controlling credit risk from a defaultable security?

    a. _____

    b. _____

    c. _____

24. What is true of the credit risk of a portfolio that is properly hedged by credit options, forwards, or swaps?

    a. It is equal to zero.

    b. It depends on the credit quality of the counterparty.

    c. It is negligible.

    d. It depends on the hedging instrument.

CHAPTER 26

Investment Companies

1. Which of the following is *not* a characteristic of open-end mutual funds?

   a. The total number of shares in the fund can change every day.

   b. Shares can trade at a discount to net asset value.

   c. Investors own a pro rata share of the overall portfolio.

   d. Net asset value depends on the number of shares outstanding.

Use this data to answer questions 2–3. The market value of a mutual fund at the beginning of the day is $300 million, and its number of shares outstanding is 20 million. It has no liabilities.

2. Calculate the net asset value of the fund at the beginning of the day.

3. At the end of the day, the market value of the portfolio has risen to $320 million. Also, at the end of the day, another $8 million is deposited in the fund. If the deposit is invested at the new NAV, what is the new number of outstanding shares? What is the new NAV at the end of the day?

4. What is true of the price of shares of a closed-end fund?

   a. It is always equal to NAV.

   b. It always trades at a premium to NAV.

   c. It always trades at a discount to NAV.

   d. The price is determined by supply and demand in the open market.

5. What is the main disadvantage in buying closed-end funds at the IPO?

   a. The initial investors bear the substantial costs of underwriting the IPO.

   b. There is usually a shortage, which causes the fund to trade at a premium to its NAV.

   c. The initial price is arbitrary because it is not set by the marketplace.

   d. It is impossible to evaluate the track record of a fund at its inception.

6. Which of the following are true of unit trusts but not true of mutual funds?

  I. A unit trust has a set termination date.

  II. A unit trust invests in bonds.

 III. A unit trust consists of a specific portfolio that rarely changes.

   a. I only

   b. III only

   c. I and III only

   d. II and III only

   e. I, II, and III

   f. None of the above

7. What are three types of sales charges on mutual funds?

   a. _____

   b. _____

   c. _____

8. What is true of mutual funds that charge a sales charge (load)?

  I. They use sales-force distribution.
  II. They give sales charge discounts for larger investors.
 III. They are generally purchased by more sophisticated investors.

   a. I only

   b. III only

   c. I and II only

d. II and III only

e. I, II, and III

9. Which of the following funds would most likely have the highest expense ratio?

   a. A bond index fund

   b. A money market fund

   c. An actively managed U.S. fund

   d. An actively managed emerging markets fund

10. Which of the following are components of the expense ratio?

   I. Front-end loads
  II. 12b-1 Fees
 III. Custodial fees

   a. I only

   b. II only

   c. I and III only

   d. II and III only

   e. I, II, and III

11. List five reasons for using mutual funds instead of investing directly.

a. _____

b. _____

c. _____

d. _____

e. _____

12. Which of the following is *not* a frequently used characteristic by which mutual funds are classified?

a. Large cap versus small cap

b. Passive management versus active management

c. Diversified versus nondiversified

d. Domestic versus international

13. Which of the following can be used to determine the exposure of a mutual fund to different types of stocks?

   I. Morningstar "Stars" Rating System
  II. Sharpe Benchmark
 III. Wall Street Journal

    a. I only

    b. II only

    c. I and II only

    d. II and III only

    e. I, II, and III

    f. None of the above

14. For investors, what is the main disadvantage of the rule that mutual funds must distribute a large percentage of their dividends and capital gains?

    a. It prevents investors from deferring their tax burden.

    b. Investors are forced to pay extra commissions if they wish to reinvest these distributions.

    c. It causes closed-end funds to sell at below NAV.

    d. All of the above

For questions 15–17, identify the following statements as *True*, *False*, or *Uncertain*. If *False* or *Uncertain*, explain briefly.

15. Funds with a load are now nonexistent because individuals refuse to pay a portion of their investment to compensate agents.

16. The SEC has enacted rules simplifying mutual fund documents and forcing disclosure of disguising practices such as window dressing.

17. The management fee is the largest part of annual operating expenses.

CHAPTER 27

Exchange-Traded Funds

1. Which of the following was the original source for the idea behind ETFs?

   a. TIPs

   b. SPDRS

   c. WEBS

   d. Program trading

2. Which of the following facts about ETFs are true?

   I. The S&P500 SPDRS ETF accounts for more than two-thirds of all ETF assets.
   II. TIPS were discontinued because they were not very popular among investors.
   III. All currently available ETFs are structured as unit investment trusts.

   a. I only

b. III only

c. I and II only

d. I and III only

e. I, II, and III

f. None of the above

3. The introduction of WEBS was important for which of the following reasons?

I. They were the foreign index funds, thus they gave investors an opportunity to gain international exposure at a very low cost.
II. They were the first ETFs traded in the secondary market.
III. They had more investment flexibility because they were structured as mutual funds, not unit investment trusts.

a. I only

b. II only

c. I and III only

d. II and III only

e. I, II, and III

f. None of the above

4. Which of the following is *not* a result of the creation-in-kind/redemption-in-kind process?

   a. Increased tax efficiency of ETFs

   b. Market price of ETFs stays close to their NAV

   c. Slightly lower transaction costs of ETFs

   d. ETFs can only used by large investors

5. What are three reasons that ETFs have a lower expense ratio than similar index funds?

   a. _____

   b. _____

   c. _____

6. Which of the following investors would find ETFs most advantageous?

   a. A day trader

   b. A long-term taxable investor who does not do dollar-cost averaging

   c. A long-term investor who frequently rebalances his portfolio

   d. A nontaxable 401k investor

7. What is the main reason that ETFs will most likely not use the unit investment trust structure in the future?

   a. The UIT structure does not allow for full replication of an index.

   b. The UIT structure does not allow for anything except full replication of an index.

   c. The UIT structure is not tax efficient.

   d. The UIT structure does not provide for in-kind creations and redemptions.

8. Which of the following are differences between open-end ETFs and HOLDRs?

  I. HOLDRs are not structured as investment companies.
  II. No HOLDRs component that disappears can be replaced.
  III. The creation unit and minimum trading unit for a HOLDR is 100 shares.

   a. I only

   b. II only

   c. I and III only

   d. II and III only

   e. I, II, and III

9. The tax efficiency of HOLDRs and Folios arises mainly from:

a. Redemption-in-kind/Creation-in-kind

b. Lower turnover of shares

c. The investor's ability to take losses in components of the basket

d. All of the above

CHAPTER 28

Real Estate Investment

1. What are the four quadrants of the modern real estate investment universe?

   a. _____

   b. _____

   c. _____

   d. _____

2. Which of the following statements is true concerning recent trends in real estate investment?

   a. The role of private debt grew in the 1980s, but shrank during the 1990s.

   b. The role of private equity has been shrinking since the early 1980s.

   c. The public debt and equity markets have played a small but growing role in recent years.

   d. REITs are now the dominant vehicle for real estate investment.

3. What are the two distinguishing characteristics of real estate?

a. _____

b. _____

4. Which of the following assets exhibit the highest level of debt-like behavior?

   a. A foreclosed mortgage

   b. A half-occupied building with many short-term tenants

   c. A vacant building

   d. A building on a long-term lease to a highly accredited tenant

5. The volatility of private equity real estate is probably:

   a. Understated by the low frequency of valuations.

   b. Low because of stable cash flows in most economic environments.

   c. Better understood because many institutional investors placed the control of valuations in the hands of independent third-parties.

   d. All of the above

6. List three reasons that the volatility of the private equity real estate market is low.

a. _____

b. _____

c. _____

7. Which of the following is true of real estate investment trusts (REITs)?

I. They are vehicles that allow a pool of real estate assets to trade in the public market.
II. They pay the regular corporate tax rate on all profits.
III. They are more leveraged than most private real estate portfolios which also makes them more volatile.

a. I only

b. II only

c. I and II only

d. I and III only

e. I, II, and III

f. None of the above

8. How are REITs likely to perform in times of stock market decline?

a. They are likely to move in the opposite direction of the stock market.

b. They are likely to move in the same direction as the stock market.

c. There is no relationship between REITs and the stock market.

d. The answer also depends on how the private real estate market is performing.

9. What are five reasons to include real estate in a portfolio?

a. _____

b. _____

c. _____

d. _____

e. _____

10. Which of the following investors would probably *not* allocate a considerable percentage of their portfolio to real estate?

   a. Long-term investors saving money for retirement

   b. Short-term investors who require a low-risk return on their money

   c. Speculators who want to gamble a small sum of money and do not care about risk

   d. Investors who are afraid that inflation will eat away the value of their portfolio

11. Which of the following descriptions of real estate's ability to hedge against inflation is true?

   a. Adding real estate to a portfolio is the best method for hedging against inflation.

   b. Publicly traded real estate equity and real estate debt are not as effective as private real estate equity in hedging against inflation.

   c. Retail is the only sector of real estate that plays any role in inflation hedging.

   d. The degree of inflation-hedging capability is uniform across all property types and quadrants of real estate investment.

12. How does real estate fit the investment needs of risk-sensitive investors?

   I. It helps diminish the overall risk of the portfolio.
   II. It helps achieve a portfolio composition similar to that of the true investment universe.
   III. More of real estate returns are composed of lower-risk cash payments.

   a. I only

   b. III only

   c. I and II only

   d. I and III only

   e. I, II, and III

13. How does leverage enhance the ability of real estate to act as a diversifier in a portfolio?

   a. It reduces the volatility of the return of the leveraged asset.

   b. It eliminates the equity-like behavior of real estate, turning it into a safe, fixed-income investment.

   c. It shorts out the debt-like behavior of real estate.

   d. All of the above

For questions 14–16, identify the following statements as *True, False,* or *Uncertain.* If *False* or *Uncertain,* explain briefly.

14. Real estate investment (except in REITs) is not for small individual investors because of prohibitive execution costs.

15. The cost approach is the best method for determining the true value of a real estate asset.

16. Real estate is a less risky asset class than bonds.

CHAPTER 29

Hedge Funds

1. Identify five differences between hedge funds and mutual funds.

   a. _____

   b. _____

   c. _____

   d. _____

   e. _____

2. Match the following hedge fund strategies with their descriptions

Strategies

1. Equity long/short hedge funds

2. Global macro hedge funds

3. Short selling hedge funds

4. Convertible bond arbitrage hedge funds

5. Fixed-income arbitrage hedge funds

6. Event driven hedge funds

7. Market neutral hedge funds

Descriptions

a. They tend to have a negative market beta.

b. They have the broadest investment universe.

c. They try to eliminate all forms of market and sector risk and concentrate on buying winners and selling losers.

d. They usually have a positive bias in net market exposure but can shift due to changing market conditions.

e. They do not make market bets but try to find mispricing in the bond markets.

f. They attempt to capture mispricing associated with capital market transactions.

g. They attempt to profit from mispricing of certain options in many corporate bonds.

3. Which of the following is *not* true about long/short hedge funds?

    a. They are similar to market neutral funds with the exception that they are allowed to have exposure to the market.

    b. They specialize in top-down analysis.

    c. They tend to have a positive beta.

    d. They may leverage their positions.

4. Which of the following events significantly hurt global macro hedge funds?

  I. The devaluation of the British pound in 1992
 II. Russian bond default in August 1998
III. Bursting of the technology bubble in 2000 and 2001

    a. II only

    b. III only

    c. I and II only

    d. II and III only

    e. I, II, and III

5. Which of these funds usually have negligible net market exposure?

  I. Convertible arbitrage funds
 II. Fixed-income arbitrage funds
III. Merger arbitrage funds

    a. I only

    b. III only

    c. I and II only

    d. II and III only

    e. I, II, and III

    f. None of the above

6. Which of the following hedge fund strategies would probably suffer the most as a result of a sudden economic downturn?

    a. Short selling

    b. Market neutral

    c. Fixed-income arbitrage

    d. Merger arbitrage

7. Volatility arbitrage involves:

   a. The purchase of equities in a low-risk environment and the sale of equities in a high-risk environment

   b. The purchase of high-duration bonds during large interest rate swings.

   c. The purchase or sale of stock options to take advantage of changes in implied volatility

   d. The purchase of call options in a high-volatility environment and the sale of put options in a low-volatility environment

8. Which of the following hedge fund managers would likely use a top-down approach?

   a. Market timing

   b. Market neutral

   c. Short selling

   d. Relative value arbitrage

9. Which of the following conclusions about hedge fund returns is supported by academic research?

I. In most cases, hedge funds are able to produce a higher risk-adjusted return, for example, a higher Sharpe Ratio, than the S&P500 Index.
II. Hedge funds are usually negatively correlated with the stock market.
III. Superior hedge fund returns are persistent. The best managers are able to consistently outperform their peers.

a. I only

b. II only

c. I and II only

d. I and III only

e. I, II, and III

f. None of the above

For questions 10–12, identify the following statements as *True*, *False*, or *Uncertain*. If *False* or *Uncertain*, explain briefly.

10. Equity long/short hedge funds are less risky than long-only mutual funds because their long and short exposures cancel out giving them a lower market beta.

11. Arbitrage funds do not take advantage of arbitrage in the economic sense of the word.

12. Analyzing their performance history is the best way of choosing hedge funds.

13. What are the three basic strategies to hedge fund investment?

    a. _____

    b. _____

    c. _____

14. What three questions are critical to understanding the nature of a hedge fund?

    a. _____

    b. _____

    c. _____

15. Identify whether each of the following hedge fund strategies achieves competitive advantage from information filtering or information gathering.

   a. A market neutral fund that uses computer modeling

   b. A health-care fund whose manager has spent thirty years doing research on this sector.

   c. A merger arbitrage fund that bets on whether mergers will or will not take place

16. Which of the following is *not* a necessary part of understanding a hedge fund manager's investment objective?

   a. The hedge fund's benchmark

   b. The hedge fund's strategy type

   c. The hedge fund's prior performance

   d. The markets in which the hedge fund tends to invest

For questions 17–18, identify the following statements as *True*, *False*, or *Uncertain*. If *False* or *Uncertain*, explain briefly.

17. An absolute return investment program requires specifying a set of parameters that govern the portfolio's risk, return, and types of strategies.

18. There is no reason to invest in a fund with a "black box" investment process because it is unlikely to do better than a fund whose process is more open.

CHAPTER 30

Private Equity

1. Which of the following companies is most likely to seek venture capital?

   a. A startup company that has run out of seed capital from family, friends, and an "angel investor"

   b. A public company that wants to avoid bankruptcy and requires restructuring capital

   c. A private company that has negative cash flows and is unable to secure bank loans to continue operations

   d. A public company that wants to go private

2. What are the main advantages of a venture capital fund of funds?

   I. There is diversification among multiple venture capitalists.
   II. Lower management fees are incurred.
   III. Venture capitalists interface with an experienced fund of funds manager instead of inexperienced investors.

a. I only

b. III only

c. I and III only

d. II and III only

e. I, II, and III

3. What is the most common method of compensation for venture capital firms?

a. Percentage fees

b. Subordinated bonds

c. Common stock

d. Preferred stock

4. Describe the seven different aspects of a company that venture capital firms will analyze when deciding whether to extend capital.

a. _____

b. _____

c. _____

d. _____

e. _____

f. _____

g. _____

5. Which of the following should be found in a company's business plan?

  I. The niche that the new company will occupy
 II. Assumptions of future revenue and profitability
III. Resources required to achieve the company's goals

   a. I only

   b. II only

   c. I and II only

   d. I and III only

   e. I, II, and III

6. Besides providing capital, identify three ways in which venture capital firms can help startup companies succeed.

   a. _____

   b. _____

   c. _____

For questions 7–9, identify the following statements as *True*, *False*, or *Uncertain*. If *False* or *Uncertain*, explain briefly.

7. Venture capitalists are able to take substantial risk in providing capital by requiring very high target rates of return.

8. Redemption rights and put options are used as a last resort exit strategy because they do not provide as high a rate of return as an acquisition or IPO.

9. A venture capital firm that raises money from a large number of passive, uninformed investors usually chooses the limited liability company structure.

10. List four ways in which venture capital firms can specialize.

a. _____

b. _____

c. _____

d. _____

Use this data to answer questions 11–15. A public company is capitalized with $1.2 billion in equity and $400 million in debt (both are market values). The company generates an annual free cash flow of $200 million.

11. What is the company's return on capital?

12. Management will perform a leveraged buyout in which it will repurchase the debt at market value, and repurchase the equity at a 20% premium over the market value. How much capital is required for the leveraged buyout?

13. After the buyout, management is able to improve operations so the company generates $250 million in free cash flows. Assuming a cash flow growth rate of 0% and a discount rate of 8%, what is (and will always be) the value of the company?

14. What was the annual rate of return on this leveraged buyout if the issued equity equaled $500 million and it took 6 years to repay the interest and principal on the remaining debt?

15. Explain the upside and downside if instead of $500 million, only $100 million in equity was issued.

16. What are four possible ways in which a LBO firm can unlock the value of a company after all the debt is paid off?

   a. _____

   b. _____

   c. _____

   d. _____

17. LBOs are less risky than venture capital deals because:

   a. LBO targets have an established operating track record.

   b. LBOs are much less capital-intensive.

   c. LBOs are less leveraged.

   d. All of the above

18. LBO firms can make money from:

I. 1%–3% in management fees from investors
II. Incentive fees in the form of profit sharing
III. Break-up fees if the deal falls through

    a. I only

    b. II only

    c. I and III only

    d. II and III only

    e. I, II, and III

    f. None of the above

19. Which of the following is a common use of mezzanine debt?

    a. To raise money to preempt bankruptcy

    b. To run the day-to-day operations of the company

    c. To fund a private company's operations before its IPO

    d. To pay out large dividends to its equityholders

20. Which of the following is *not* a characteristic of mezzanine funds?

   a. Mezzanine funds take on less risk than LBO firms and venture capital firms.

   b. Investors in mezzanine funds are usually large private investors.

   c. Mezzanine lenders often have some say in company decisions, and may even have board observation rights or full voting rights.

   d. Mezzanine funds are more interested in a company's future growth and success than in conventional banking parameters such as collateral.

21. What is a likely reason for investing in mezzanine debt?

   a. Stable cash flows with little or no risk

   b. High coupon returns with a possible equity stake in the company if it expands.

   c. Excellent opportunity for extremely high rates of return

   d. Ability to make money from turning around a failed company

22. What is the major effect of a spike in interest rates on distressed debt?

   a. The distressed debt falls in price as its cash flows are discounted at a higher rate.

   b. The distressed debt rises in price as its equity share gains value.

   c. There is little or no effect because the value of the debt will depend on the success or failure of the company.

   d. There is little or no effect because distressed debt cash flows already reflect higher interest rates in their yield.

23. Which of the following are important risks of investing in distressed debt?

 I. Credit risk
 II. Business risk
 III. Liquidity risk

   a. II only

   b. III only

   c. I and III only

   d. II and III only

   e. I, II, and III

   f. None of the above

For questions 24–26, identify the following statements as *True, False,* or *Uncertain.* If *False* or *Uncertain,* explain briefly.

24. Leveraged buyout allow management to improve the efficiency of the firm.

25. Mezzanine debt usually returns at least as much as the firm's equity.

26. Firms conduct distressed debt arbitrage by selling the distressed company's debt and buying the distressed company's stock.

CHAPTER 31

Active Asset Allocation

1. Identify whether each of the following descriptions pertains to policy asset allocation, tactical asset allocation, both, or neither.

   a. Sometimes called strategic asset allocation

   b. Inherently a "buy low, sell high" process

   c. An active strategy

   d. Balances long-term risks and rewards of different asset classes

   e. Can be used in conjunction with rebalancing

   f. Also called dynamic asset allocation

2. What are some problems with optimization techniques for asset allocation?

  I. They may suggest portfolios that the investor, for other reasons, is unwilling to hold.

 II. They are vulnerable to small errors in estimates of future expected returns, variances, and covariances among the asset classes.

III. They are not as intuitive as a simple tactical framework.

    a. I only

    b. III only

    c. I and III only

    d. II and III only

    e. I, II, and III

    f. None of the above

3. What is true of policy asset allocation?

    a. It depends on type of investor and the time horizon.

    b. It requires the minimization of volatility as the main risk.

    c. It utilizes mean-variance optimization.

    d. All of the above

4. A portfolio has a 60% normal allocation to stocks with a 4% range. Assuming that on January 15, the allocation to stocks was 67%, when and how will the portfolio be rebalanced under each of the following frameworks?

   a. Calendar rebalancing done at the end of each quarter

   b. Rebalancing to allowed range

   c. Threshold rebalancing

   d. Drifting mix

5. Tactical asset allocation is based on:

   a. Using historical returns to allocate to the asset class with the best performance.

   b. Rotating in and out of different asset classes depending on their relative attractiveness of future returns.

   c. Choosing a position in different asset classes to meet long-term risk and reward targets.

   d. Rebalancing one's entire portfolio to prevent slippage.

6. Identify four important questions that need to be addressed by a good asset allocation strategy.

   a. _____

   b. _____

   c. _____

   d. _____

7. Which of the following are characteristics of most tactical asset allocation strategies?

I. They enhance portfolio performance.
II. They are contrarian in nature.
III. They are only designed to capture short-term movements in the markets.

a. I only

b. III only

c. I and II only

d. II and III only

e. I, II, and III

8. Identify six advantages of using futures to implement an asset allocation strategy.

a. _____

b. _____

c. _____

d. _____

e. _____

f. _____

9. Identify three disadvantages of using futures to implement an asset allocation strategy.

   a. _____

   b. _____

   c. _____

For questions 10–13, identify the following statements as *True*, *False*, or *Uncertain*. If *False* or *Uncertain*, explain briefly.

10. Portfolio insurance is a policy asset allocation strategy that seeks to minimize losses over a long-term period.

11. Periodic rebalancing is essential to maintaining the chosen risk and return profile of a portfolio.

12. Discipline is one of the key benefits of strictly implementing a tactical asset allocation strategy.

13. Asset allocation strategies improve the quality of securities in each asset class in the portfolio.

Solutions

Investment Management

1. a. Setting investment objectives

   b. Establishing an investment policy

   c. Selecting an investment strategy

   d. Selecting the specific assets

   e. Measuring and evaluating investment performance

2. (a) The other three are institutional investors who often have outlays at specific times that they must meet.

3. a. U.S. government bonds are a subdivision of the U.S. bonds asset class.

   b. Standard & Poor's 500 is a benchmark index for the U.S. stocks (large-cap) asset class.

   c. Hedge funds are an alternative investments asset class.

   d. Real estate is a traditional asset class.

   e. U.S. growth stocks are a subdivision of the U.S. stocks asset class.

   f. Emerging market stocks are a subdivision of the foreign stocks asset class.

g. Mortgage-backed securities are a subdivision of the U.S. bonds asset class.

h. Salomon Brothers Broad is a benchmark index for the U.S. bonds asset class.

4. Uncertain—market capitalization equals number of shares multiplied by the stock price. The statement is only true if stock price equals 1.

5. False—mutual funds allow small investors to have exposure to a broad asset class.

6. False—tax policy might influence the after-tax earnings of companies whose stocks are in the portfolio of a tax-exempt investor making them more or less attractive.

7. True

8. (f) None of the statements are good reasons. The first two would be reasons to choose an active over a passive investment strategy. The last one is always true and not a reason to choose either passive or active over the other.

9. a. Expected return (or future expected return) can be estimated from various asset pricing models or from historical data. Investors also can use intuition to estimate this input.

   b. Variance of asset returns can be estimated by looking at historical variance. This estimate can be improved through sophisticated time series statistical techniques.

   b. Covariance (or correlation) of returns is typically obtained from historical data.

10. (c)

11. (c), by definition

CHAPTER 2

Portfolio Selection

1. $E(R) = p_1 R_1 + p_2 R_2 + p_3 R_3 + p_4 R_4$

   $E(R_{\text{LMN}}) = (0.15)(12\%) + (0.40)(7\%) + (0.35)(4\%) + (0.10)(0\%)$
   $= 6\%$

   $E(R_{\text{OPQ}}) = (0.15)(-2\%) + (0.40)(6\%) + (0.35)(4\%) + (0.10)(25\%)$
   $= 6\%$

   Both assets have an expected return of 6%.

2. $\text{var}(R) = p_1[r_1 - E(R)]^2 + p_2[r_2 - E(R)]^2 + p_3[r_3 - E(R)]^2$
   $+ p_4[r_4 - E(R)]^2$

   $\text{var}(R_{\text{LMN}}) = 0.15(12\% - 6\%)^2 + 0.40(7\% - 6\%)^2 + 0.35(4\% - 6\%)^2$
   $+ 0.10(0\% - 6\%)^2$
   $= 10.8\%$

   $\text{SD}(R_{\text{LMN}}) = \sqrt{\text{var}(R_{\text{LMN}})} = \sqrt{(10.8\%)} = 3.3\%$

   $\text{var}(R_{\text{OPQ}}) = 0.15(-2\% - 6\%)^2 + 0.40(6\% - 6\%)^2 + 0.35(4\% - 6\%)^2$
   $+ 0.10(25\% - 6\%)^2$
   $= 47.1\%$

   $\text{SD}(R_{\text{OPQ}}) = \sqrt{\text{var}(R_{\text{OPQ}})} = \sqrt{(47.1\%)} = 6.9\%$

   Asset OPQ is riskier because it has a higher variance (and standard deviation) than asset LMN.

3. $\text{cov}(R_i, R_j) = p_1[r_{i1} - E(R_i)][r_{j1} - E(R_j)] + p_2[r_{i2} - E(R_i)][r_{j2} - E(R_j)]$
$\qquad + p_3[r_{i3} - E(R_i)][r_{j3} - E(R_j)] + p_4[r_{i4} - E(R_i)][r_{j4} - E(R_j)]$

$\text{cov}(R_{LMN}, R_{OPQ}) = 0.15(12\% - 6\%)(-2\% - 6\%) + 0.40(7\% - 6\%)(6\% - 6\%)$
$\qquad\qquad + 0.35(4\% - 6\%)(4\% - 6\%) + 0.10(0\% - 6\%)(25\% - 6\%)$
$\qquad\qquad = -17.2$

$\text{cor}(R_{LMN}, R_{OPQ}) = \text{cov}(R_{LMN}, R_{OPQ})/[\text{SD}(R_{LMN})\ \text{SD}(R_{OPQ})]$
$\qquad\qquad = -17.2\%/[(3.3\%)(6.9\%)]$
$\qquad\qquad = -0.76$

The assets move in opposite directions because they have negative covariance (and correlation).

4. $E(R_p) = w_{LMN}E(R_{LMN}) + w_{OPQ}E(R_{OPQ}) = (0.6)(6\%) + (0.4)(6\%)$
$\qquad = 6\%$

$$\text{var}(R_p) = w_{LMN}^2 \text{var}(R_{LMN}) + w_{OPQ}^2 \text{var}(R_{OPQ})$$
$$+ 2(w_{LMN})(w_{OPQ})\text{cov}(R_{LMN}, R_{OPQ})$$

$\text{var}(R_p) = 0.6^2(10.8\%) + 0.4^2(47.1\%) + (2)(0.6)(0.4)(-17.2\%) = 3.168\%$

$$\text{SD}(R_p) = \sqrt{\text{var}(R_p)} = \sqrt{(3.168\%)} = 1.8\%$$

5. No, it's not efficient. By increasing the amount of percentage of asset LMN to 70% (and decreasing that of OPQ to 30%), we obtain:

$E(R_p) = w_{LMN}E(R_{LMN}) + w_{OPQ}E(R_{OPQ}) = (0.7)(6\%) + (0.3)(6\%)$
$\qquad = 6\%$

$\text{var}(R_p) = 0.7^2(10.8\%) + 0.3^2(47.1\%) + (2)(0.7)(0.3)(-17.2\%)$
$\qquad = 2.307\%$

This portfolio has the same expected return but lower variance so it dominates the other portfolio.

6. First, we notice that $w_{LMN} + w_{OPQ} = 1$ because the percentages must add to 100. Thus, we can substitute $1 - w_{LMN}$ for w_{OPQ} in the variance equation.

$$\mathrm{var}(R_p) = w_{\mathrm{LMN}}2\, \mathrm{var}(R_{\mathrm{LMN}}) + (1 - w_{\mathrm{LMN}})^2\, \mathrm{var}(R_{\mathrm{OPQ}})$$
$$+ 2(w_{\mathrm{LMN}})(1 - w_{\mathrm{LMN}})\, \mathrm{cov}(R_{\mathrm{LMN}}, R_{\mathrm{OPQ}})$$

Now, we can either graph the variance as w_{LMN} goes from 0 to 1 or we can differentiate with respect to w_{LMN}.

Differentiating and setting equal to zero to get the minimum variance, we find that the optimal share of asset LMN is:

$$w_{\mathrm{LMN}} = [2\mathrm{var}(R_{\mathrm{OPQ}}) - 2\mathrm{cov}(R_{\mathrm{LMN}}, R_{\mathrm{OPQ}})]/$$
$$[2\mathrm{var}(R_{\mathrm{LMN}}) + 2\mathrm{var}(R_{\mathrm{OPQ}}) - 4\mathrm{cov}(R_{\mathrm{LMN}}, R_{\mathrm{OPQ}})]$$

$$w_{\mathrm{LMN}} = [2(47.1\%) - 2(-17.2\%)]/[2(10.8\%) + 2(47.1\%) - 4(-17.2\%)]$$
$$= 0.697$$

Thus, the optimal portfolio has 69.7% of asset LMN and 30.3% of asset OPQ.

7. One of the key principles of Markowitz diversification is that it is possible to lower portfolio risk by combining assets with low or negative correlations. In this case, by adding asset OPQ to our portfolio, we can lower its variance (without hurting expected return), even though asset LMN is superior to OPQ (has same expected return but lower variance).

8. False—it simply means that indifference curves have to be drawn approximately. In other words, an investor has to subjectively choose which efficient portfolio is optimal given his or her tolerance for risk.

9. True

10. False—the beta of a portfolio is the weighted average of the betas of the constituents so it can't be greater than all the constituents unless one or more of the constituents have a weight greater than 1.

11. False—all points on the same indifference curve indicate combinations of risk and expected return that give the same level of utility to a given investor.

12. (d) All three could cause two investors to have two different optimal portfolios.

13. (a) I is true. II is false because variances can be estimated from historical data. III is false because there is an actual formula that allows computers to do this quickly with all the inputs. IV is also false, and is a reason why semivariance wasn't used by Markowitz.

14. (d) Short-term U.S. government obligations are considered risk-free.

15. All points on or inside the curve (gray area) are feasible portfolios.

16. All points on curve between points II and III are on the efficiency frontier.

17. No, we need the set of indifference curves, because then we are able to find the tangency between an indifference curve and the efficiency frontier. This point is the optimal portfolio.

18. (b), by definition

CHAPTER 3

Applying Mean-Variance Analysis

1. Index ABC has the most stable figures over the two periods, and it also has the lowest standard deviation which suggests that its parameters are more reliable over time.

2. (e), The first statement would explain the bad performance of Index DEF over the last four years, and would suggest that its annualized return may revert to the levels of 1995 to 1998 once more normal conditions ensue. This might make us overweigh DEF but certainly wouldn't make us underweigh it. The second statement has nothing to do with the Markowitz model of choice because the asset classes are already defined by the parameters of expected return and standard deviation. The third statement might make us underweigh GHI (and raise the weights of the other two indices) because of its bad performance in the past, but this wouldn't cause us to underweigh DEF unless we knew that they were highly correlated. Thus, I and III would probably make us decide to overweigh DEF, and II would have no effect. The answer is None of the above.

3. (d)

4. a. One method is to impose constraints on the maximum exposure of the asset classes represented by those indexes.

   b. Another method is to increase the input for standard deviation to account for the uncertainty in the expected return estimates.

c. Another method is to use personal judgment underpinned by expectations of the future political and economic environments of the countries represented by those indexes to adjust the inputs.

5. $(22 - 20)/20 = 10\%$. We assume that there were no dividends or stock splits during the month for this number to be correct.

6. For several reasons, the first estimate is likely to be far more precise than the second one. One reason is that we have a longer history of performance for U.S. bonds. Another reason is that the United States has a long history of free markets and property rights and is a developed country, while Algeria is a developing country without that stability. Finally, bonds, as an asset class, are generally less volatile than stocks, which makes prediction of their returns more precise.

7. They are all equally risky (they all have the same standard deviation).

8. An investor might choose Portfolio X″ instead of Portfolio X′ because he or she wants to limit exposure to the unfamiliar international equity asset class. The trade-off is that by limiting this exposure, the investor loses 33 basis points (from 10.55% to 10.22%) of expected return.

9. (c) Adding assets can only improve expected return because it is always possible to have a weight of zero on any new assets (i.e., not using them in one's portfolio).

10. a. Active funds charge higher fees than passive index funds so it is important to consider net-of-fees returns when deciding whether to implement an active strategy.

b. It is difficult to select an outperforming mutual fund because many winners in previous years will be losers in the future. Active funds in some asset classes (such as international equity) are less consistent than other classes.

c. Active strategies are often more risky than the asset classes they represent because they can be more concentrated than the well-diversified indexes.

d. Sometimes active funds gain exposure to securities outside their asset class so it becomes necessary to correct for these biases. This is possible with Sharpe's technique which doesn't require fund holdings but easily accessible fund returns.

11. Uncertain—there is a trade-off between rebalancing often to keep the weights close to optimal and keeping down trading costs. Thus, there is no best frequency at which one should rebalance.

12. True

CHAPTER 4

Asset Pricing Models

1. Zero and zero. Short-term U.S. government bonds are considered risk-free and earn the risk-free rate with no premium. Their expected returns have no variance as they are known beforehand.

2. 10%. Risk premium equals the beta multiplied by the market premium.

3. 16%. Expected return equals risk premium plus the risk-free rate.

4. The sole source of risk in the CAPM is market risk. It is systematic because it can not be diversified away.

5. (e) The first statement undermines Assumption 3, the second undermines Assumption 6, the third undermines Assumption 5.

6. (a) The first statement is true by definition. The second statement is false because the CML is a set of portfolios with betas varying from 0 (the risk-free asset) to infinity (infinitely leveraged). The third statement is also false. The beta of portfolio M equals 1. The risk premium of the CML is $[E(R_M) - R_f][\text{SD}(R_p)/\text{SD}(R_M)]$.

7. True

8. True

9. False—Both the Treynor measure and Jensen measure assume that the portfolio is well diversified and that there is only systematic risk.

10. Treynor measure: Portfolio A is better

    Portfolio A: $(11\% - 5\%)/1.25 = 4.8\%$
    Portfolio B: $(15\% - 5\%)/2.5 = 4.0\%$

    Sharpe measure: Portfolio B is better

    Portfolio A: $(11\% - 5\%)/30\% = 0.2$
    Portfolio B: $(15\% - 5\%)/25\% = 0.4$

    Jensen measure: Portfolio A is better

    Portfolio A: 1%
    Portfolio B: 0%

    Different measures give different results.

11. Portfolio B is dominant under Markowitz because it has a higher return and a lower standard deviation. However, CAPM says that only systematic risk matters because unsystematic risk can be diversified away. Portfolio A has a lower level of systematic risk so it is superior from the standpoint of CAPM (Treynor and Jensen measures).

12. Portfolio A has lower systematic risk than portfolio B (lower beta), but has higher total risk than portfolio B (higher standard deviation). The only way that this is possible is if Portfolio A has higher nonsystematic risk.

13. 9% – Market return = Risk-free rate + Market premium = 5% + 4%

14. First, they found that stocks with low beta outperform the predictions of the CAPM and stocks with high beta underperform the predictions of the CAPM. They also found that market risk isn't the only risk factor priced by the market, but that there are other factors that explain stock returns.

    Richard Roll challenged these studies when he showed that the CAPM is not testable until the composition of the true market portfolio is known. Because of the inability to observe the true market portfolio, there will never be a way to definitely prove or disprove the model.

15. a. Fischer Black examined how the CAPM is affected by eliminating Assumption 6 (i.e., that there is a risk-free rate at which investors can borrow and lend as much as they want). He demonstrated that Assumption 6 isn't necessary for the CAPM to hold by forming a "zero-beta portfolio" whose return can be substituted for the risk-free rate without fundamentally altering the results of the CAPM.

b. Robert Merton altered the CAPM by looking at other risks that investors are concerned with such as future wages and future prices of consumer goods. He based his modifications on consumers deriving their optimal lifetime consumption facing such nonmarket risks.

16. The beta in the market model is used simply as a proxy measure of covariance with an index so that one doesn't need the full variance-covariance matrix for Markowitz portfolio selection. The index need not be a market portfolio and the returns are not adjusted by the risk-free rate. The beta in the CAPM is used to measure the systematic risk of a portfolio in comparison to the market portfolio. The returns are adjusted for the risk-free rate, so we are comparing the risk premiums. The confusion about the distinction between these two betas has led to incorrect statements about the drawbacks of the CAPM.

17. Payoff in state 1 is $(5)(\$4) + (7)(\$5) = \$20 + \$35 = \$55$
Payoff in state 2 is $(5)(\$6) + (7)(\$5) = \$30 + \$35 = \$65$
Note that these are the same payoffs as from one share of Asset C.

18. The cost is $(5)(\$2.20) + (7)(\$2) = \$11 + \$14 = \$25$

19. There is an arbitrage opportunity. By buying the portfolio above (for $25) and selling short one share of Asset C (for $30), you make $5 no matter which state actually occurs and without any risk.

20. Portfolio A's expected return = $3\% + (0.7)(5\%) + (0.8)(4\%) + (0.1)(9\%)$
   $= 10.6\%$
Portfolio B's expected return = $3\% + (0.6)(5\%) + (1.3)(4\%) + (1.1)(9\%)$
   $= 21.1\%$
Portfolio C's expected return = $3\% + (0.3)(5\%) + (0)(4\%) + (1.7)(9\%)$
   $= 19.8\%$

21. a. Statistical factor models determine factors using statistical analysis and then attempt to determine their economic meaning.

b. Macroeconomic factor models try to explain returns using important macroeconomic variables.

c. Fundamental factor models try to explain returns using company and industry vital statistics such as P/E ratios, and the like.

CHAPTER 5

Calculating Investment Returns

1. a. The rate of return compresses a large amount of data about the portfolio into one simple statistic.

   b. A ratio is easier to understand and analyze than large absolute numbers.

   c. Returns are comparable among different portfolios or investors.

   d. Returns are comparable over different time periods.

   e. The interpretation of the rate of return number is intuitive. Given any amount invested, an investor can take the return and use it to determine the amount of money at the end of the period.

2. Return = (Gain or loss)/(Investment made) × 100
   = ($12 − $10)/($10) × 100 = 20%

3. Return (with no accrued income)
   = [(End market value)/(Beginning market value) − 1] × 100
   = [($12/$10) − 1] × 100 = 20%

4. There is no difference. Rates of return don't treat these two questions differently.

5. Return = [(End market value + Ending accrued income)/
             (Beginning market value) − 1] × 100
   = [(($12 + $1)/$10) −1] × 100 = 30%

6. It does not change anything. Whether gains are realized or not, the rate of return is not affected.

7. (c) This change occurs because of market conditions and not because of contributions or withdrawals to inventory.

8. (c) The return on investment includes cash flows but doesn't take into account their timing. The MWR needs timing explicitly, and the TWR needs the timing of cash flows in order to subdivide the return into periods.

9. ROI = [(EMV + NOF) – (BMV + NIF)/(BMV + NIF)] × 100
    = [(1,000 + 400) – (1,000 + 400)/(1,000 + 400)] × 100 = 0%

10. $MVE = MVB \times (1 + IRR) + CF_1 \times (1 + IRR)^m + CF_2 \times (1 + IRR)^n$

$1,400 = \$1,000 \times (1 + IRR) + \$100 \times (1 + IRR)^{7/12} + \$300 \times (1 + IRR)^{5/12}$

End value is $1,400 ($1,000 in stock and $400 in cash). The initial $1,000 was invested for the whole year. The $100 cash flow was invested for 7 out of 12 months (April–October) and the $300 cash flow was invested for 5 out of 12 months (June–October). Solving this equation gives IRR = 0%.

11. The Modified Dietz return = 0%. We only need to look at the numerator: MVE – MVB – CF = ($1,000 – $1,000 – $0) = $0.
    CF is net cash flow which is zero. Because the numerator is zero, we know the return also equals zero.

12. Subdivide the year into four periods.

Jan 1 – Mar 31:   Return = ($800 – $1,000)/($1,000)   = –20%
Apr 1 – May 31:   Return = ($1,200 – $900)/($900)   = 33.33%
Jun 1 – Oct 31:   Return = ($1,700 – $1,500)/($1,500) = 13.33%
Nov 1 – Dec 31:   Return = ($1,000 – $1,300)/($1,300) = –23.08%

Now, we do geometric linking: (0.8)(1.3333)(1.1333)(0.7692) = 0.9298
(0.9298 – 1) × 100 = –7.02%

13. The TWR is negative but the investor didn't actually lose any money over the year. The reason for this is that the investor managed to buy

low and sell high, which offset the negative performance on the manager's part.

14. The IRR is a money-weighted return which means it incorporates the decisions of both the manager and the investor. The major disadvantage of the IRR is that it is not possible to calculate explicitly. The Modified Dietz return can be used as an MWR if the IRR is too difficult to determine.

    The TWR, or time-weighted return, isolates the decisions of the manager and allows investors to measure the performance of the manager without the interference of investor timing decisions. The major disadvantage of TWR is that it requires valuations at each cash flow. The linked MWR is a method of estimating the TWR without this valuation data.

15. $[(1.10)(1.15)(1.40) - 1] \times 100 = 77.1\%$

16. Arithmetic mean = Sum(Periodic return)/# of returns used
    $$= (10\% + 15\% + 40\%)/3$$
    $$= 21.7\%$$

17. Geometric mean = $[\sqrt[N]{1 + \text{Cumulative Return}} - 1] \times 100$

    $$= (1.771^{\frac{1}{3}}) - 1 \times 100$$
    $$= 21.0\%$$

18. (a)

19. $1.2^{(2/3)} = 1.129$
    $$= 12.9\% \text{ annualized return}$$

CHAPTER 6

Common Stock Markets, Trading Arrangements, and Trading Costs

1. 1-d, 2-g, 3-c, 4-i, 5-b, 6-e, 7-a, 8-h, 9-f

2. (c) The third market refers to trading of exchange-listed stocks over the counter.

3. (a) While it is true that mostly small-cap stocks are traded on the OTC, and that there is no central trading floor, there are actually far more stocks traded on the OTC than on the NYSE.

4. (d) There can be more than one specialist at each post.

5. (b) ECNs are actually more effective for handling smaller orders.

6. (c) Market makers are only allowed to trade stock for their own account if the trades are necessary to ensure a fair and orderly market.

7. (e) All the statements are true.

8. a. Instinet is both an ECN and operates a crossing network.

   b. Pink Sheets are an OTC market.

   c. ITG Posit is a crossing network.

    d. AMEX, the American Stock Exchange, is an exchange.

    e. Archipelago is an ECN.

    f. Nasdaq is an OTC market.

9. a. stop order

    b. limit order

    c. market order

    d. stop-limit order

    e. fill or kill order

    f. market if touched order

10. a. The major disadvantage of the market order is that you have no control of the price you will get. Thus, any major moves between the time you place the order and the time that it gets executed can make a large difference.

    b. The major disadvantage of the limit order is that it may never get executed at all.

    c. The major disadvantages of the stop order are that the price may hit the target and then bounce back resulting in a premature trade. Furthermore, it turns into a market order when the trigger is reached so it suffers all the problems of the market order.

11. She can buy $1,000/$10 = 100 shares of XYZ.
Her profit will be (100 shares) ($5/Share price increase) = $500
Return = Profit/Initial equity = ($500)/($1,000) = 50%

12. She can invest $1,000 and borrow $2,000 (for an initial margin of 1/3).
This would buy her $3,000/$10 = 300 shares of XYZ
Her profit will be (300 shares) ($5/share price increase) = $1,500
She must pay interest on the loan equal to (5%)($2,000) = $100 so her remaining profit is $1,500 − $100 = $1,400
Return = Profit/Initial equity = ($1,400)/($1,000) = 140%

13. She would buy 300 shares of XYZ. Their value would drop to ($7)(300 shares) = $2,100. She would have to pay $100 in interest payments and return the loan of $2,000. This would leave her with $0 in equity.

14. She must add $100 to pay the interest. She also will have to add $400 in cash. Her account will then have $2,100 in stock, $400 in cash for a total of $2,500 of which $2,000 (4/5ths) is margin and the remaining $500 (1/5th) is equity. Thus, she must add a total of $500.

15. (a) The investor doesn't need to own the shares to be sold short because they are borrowed. Also, the proceeds are not required to be reinvested or removed, but usually stay as collateral to allow the broker to buy back the shares and return them to the borrower.

16. (d) Taxes are explicit costs. Not making a trade is an opportunity cost and is implicit. Impact costs are also implicit.

17. Price limits were first used in the stock market in the aftermath of the 1987 crash. They are mainly used to calm emotions in order to prevent stock market panics like the one that occurred in 1987.

18. False—only small orders have become cheaper. Larger, more difficult trades have not seen lower commissions.

19. True

20. Uncertain—while the second statement is true, the counterbalancing argument is that payments for order flow may divert retail orders from going to the best markets. Whether payments for order flow are good for investors remains controversial.

21. False—pretrade benchmarks are actually easy to implement by simply comparing the price after the transaction to a pretrade price. Their real disadvantage is that they can be rigged.

22. (a) Discount brokers have caused explicit costs (i.e., commissions) to come down. It is difficult to say whether implicit costs have also been coming down.

23. a. Retail trades are usually smaller than institutional trades. Institutions often make large block or program trades.

b. Institutions usually pay lower commissions than retail investors.

c. Retail investors usually trade through their stockbroker and their trades go to the retail exchange execution desk. Institutions move their trades directly to the institutional broker-dealer exchange execution desk.

24. (b) A is false because program trades are cheaper than doing each individual trade are one at a time. C is false because agency program trades minimize commissions but may have high implicit costs. D is false because agency incentive agreements give the investor a threshold for the price and commission, but not the exact price.

25. They can use stock index futures with similar characteristics to the portfolio to protect themselves from movements in the market.

26. a. Benchmarks for evaluating the performance of money managers

    b. Encapsulate the performance of a large group of stocks in one number

27. a. Nasdaq Composite

    b. S&P 500, Nasdaq Composite, Wilshire 5000

    c. Dow Jones Industrial Average

    d. Wilshire 5000

    e. S&P 500, Dow Jones Industrial Average

28. (e), All the statements are true.

29. (d), Stricter capital flow restrictions would lower correlations by preventing money from leaving developing countries during financial crises.

30. a. Corporations do not have to comply with issuing regulations of the foreign country where the stock will be traded.

    b. Investors can trade on the domestic market during domestic hours.

    c. Investors receive and make payments in domestic currency.

CHAPTER 7

Tracking Error and Common Stock Portfolio Management

1. For Manager A, the active return in year 1 is 12% − 10% = 2%
   The active return in year 2 is 10% − 8% = 2%
   The active return in year 3 is 9% − 7% = 2%
   For Manager B, the active return in year 1 is 12% − 10% = 2%
   The active return in year 2 is 15% − 8% = 7%
   The active return in year 3 is 4% − 7% = −3%

2. Alpha is the average active return.
   For Manager A, the alpha = (2% + 2% + 2%)/3 = 2%
   For Manager B, the alpha = (2% + 7% − 3%)/3 = 2%

3. The tracking error of Manager A is 0%.
   The tracking error of Manager B is the square root of:
   $(1/3) [(2\% - 2\%)^2 + (7\% - 2\%)^2 + (-3 - 2\%)^2] = 1/3[0 + 25 + 25]$
   = Tracking error of Manager B is square root of 16.7
   = 4.08%

4. Information Ratio of Manager A is 2%/0% = infinity
   Information Ratio of Manager B is 2%/4.08% = 0.49
   Clearly, Manager A is doing a better job because his alpha is the same as that of Manager B but he achieves it with no tracking error. Thus, he has a higher information ratio.

5. The tracking error of that portfolio is 10% × 4.08% = 0.41%

6. (a) The first statement is false because ex-post tracking error is another name for backward-looking tracking error. The third statement is false because there is no guarantee that the predicted (forward-looking) tracking error will be identical to the actual backward-looking tracking error in the future.

7. (c) The quarterly variance is 25%. The quarterly standard deviation is 5% (square root of 25). The yearly standard deviation, which is the annual tracking error, is $5\% \times \sqrt{4} = 10\%$. We have to multiply by the square root of 4 because there are four quarters in each year.

8. (f) Each of the three events would actually cause tracking error to fall.

9. (c) The S&P500 has a blend of growth and value stocks so by having a blend of them in your portfolio, you would decrease its tracking error.

10. A 3% increase in exposure caused a 6% decrease in tracking error. Thus, the marginal contribution to tracking error is –2%.

11. No, first because the rate calculated in question 10 only holds at the margin. Second, after the sector becomes overweighted (goes above 9%), the marginal contribution will become positive.

12. a. The CIO can ask that manager to decrease tracking error.

    b. The CIO can reduce the allocation to that asset class.

    c. The CIO can try to alter the correlation structure between that portfolio and other portfolios.

CHAPTER 8

Common Stock Portfolio Management Strategies

1. False—investment management is actually a complicated, integrated process that must be implemented in a cost-efficient manner.

2. Uncertain—this depends on the form of efficiency. While it's likely true that the market is weak-form efficient and perhaps even semis-trong-form efficient, evidence suggests that the market is probably not strong-form efficient.

3. True

4. a. Alpha

   b. Tracking error

5. (c) Investors who don't believe that the stock market is efficient are much more likely to do active portfolio management.

6. (d), by definition

7. (c) The first two statements are true. The last statement is false because value managers expect the price-to-book ratio and the price itself to go up.

8. a. Low P/E managers concentrate on companies that trade at low prices relative to their earnings.

b. Contrarian managers concentrate on depressed companies that have low prices compared to their book value.

c. Yield managers, the most conservative value managers, concentrate on stocks with high dividend yields.

9. a. Consistent growth managers focus on high-quality companies with a long record of growing earnings.

b. Earnings momentum growth managers focus on more volatile companies with high growth in expectation that their growth will accelerate.

10. (b) The first statement is false because "size" refers to the size of the fund's constituents, not the size of the fund itself. The third statement is false because there are only 9 (3×3 matrix) possible classifications under the Morningstar system.

11. a. One approach is to buy all the stocks in the index in proportion to their weightings.

b. A second approach, known as the capitalization approach, is to buy the largest capitalized stocks and distribute the rest equally among the other index constituents.

c. A third approach is to buy fewer stocks than are in the index through the cellular method. This involves defining risk factors to which the stocks in the index are exposed, and then diversifying in the same proportion as the index.

d. A fourth approach is to buy fewer stocks than are in the index and to use a multi-factor risk model to match the risk profile of the index.

12. (d)

13. a. Fundamental

b. Technical

c. Fundamental

d. Neither (top-down analysis)

    e. Fundamental

    f. Technical

14. (e)

15. (d) The first three are more often used in fundamental analysis.

16. (a)

CHAPTER 9

Traditional Fundamental Analysis I: Sources of Information

1. a. 10-K filing with the Securities and Exchange Commission

   b. Annual report to shareholders

   c. Interviewing company representatives

   d. EDGAR system on the SEC Web site

   e. Financial service companies' databases such as Compustat

   f. Most major newspapers' financial pages

2. a. Play the role of a referee in terms of securities rules.

   b. Require disclosure to make public companies more transparent.

   c. Issue statements concerning current issues.

   d. Oversee exchanges and bodies, such as the NASD, which self-regulate the securities industry.

3. (d) The first statement isn't true.

4. (b)

5. (a) While the other three events may prompt the company to issue an 8-K, only bankruptcy forces the issue.

6. (c) The letter to shareholders is usually just an investor-friendly version of the MDA, and any misleading statements in it will not be taken as seriously as misleading statements in official SEC filings.

7. a. Restatement of prior years' data may indicate a change in accounting practices or corrections due to error or fraud.

   b. Off-balance-sheet activity may expose the company to substantial risks and requires careful inspection of all footnotes, addendums, and the like.

   c. Pro forma financial data must be analyzed to see what assumptions were made and then recalculated in GAAP terms to allow comparisons across companies and time.

8. (d) NAICS is not simple and unambiguous because there are many companies that are involved in multiple industries.

9. (a)

10. False—they are used to provide additional information and insight into the company's business.

11. True

CHAPTER 10

Traditional Fundamental Analysis II: Financial Ratio Analysis

1. a. None of the above

   a. Return ratio

   b. Coverage ratio

   c. Component percentage ratio

   d. None of the above

   e. Component percentage ratio

   f. Turnover ratio

2. The gross profit of the company is:

   Sales − Cost of goods sold = $30,000 − $16,000 = $14,000

   Thus the gross profit margin is:

   Gross profit/Sales = $14,000/$30,000 = 0.47 or 47%

   The operating profit of the company is:

Gross profit – Operating expenses = $14,000 – $4,000 = $10,000

Thus, the operating profit margin is:

Operating profit/Sales = $10,000/$30,000 = 0.33 or 33%

The net profit of the company is:

Operating profit – Taxes – Interest = $10,000 – $2,000 – $1,000 = $7,000

Thus, the net profit margin is:

Net profit/Sales = $7,000/$30,000 = 0.23 or 23%

3. Basic earnings power = Operating profit/Total assets
   = $10,000/$50,000 = 0.20 or 20%

Return on assets = Net income/Total assets
   = $7,000/$50,000 = 0.14 or 14%

4. (b) The second statement is *not* implied. We know neither the book value nor the market value of equity so we are unable to make any statements about returns to shareholders on their investments.

5. (b)

6. Total credit sales equal half of all sales which equals (0.5)($30,000) = $15,000

Average day's credit sales equals $15,000/365 = $41.10 p/day

Average day's cost of goods sold equals $16,000/365 = $43.84 p/day

7. Number of days of inventory = Inventory/Average day's cost of goods sold = $5,000/$43.84 = 114 days

Number of days of credit = Accounts Receivable/Average day's credits sales = $2,000/$41.10 = 49 days

8. Operating cycle = Number of days of inventory + number of days of credit = 114 + 49 = 163 days

Net operating cycle = Operating cycle – Number of days of payables
= 163 – 30 = 133 days

9. (d) Its quick ratio excludes inventories from current assets and is equal to 1.

10. Activity ratios are used to evaluate the benefits produced by specific assets or the firm's total assets.

   a. The inventory turnover ratio indicates how a company uses its inventory to create sales.

   b. The accounts receivable turnover ratio measures how a firm is using credit.

   c. The total assets turnover ratio tells us how many times during the year the value of a firm's total assets is generated in sales.

   d. The fixed assets turnover ratio is similar to the fixed asset turnover ratio but uses only the firm's long-term tangible assets.

   Activity ratios don't tell us the number of sales not made because credit policies are too stringent, how much of credit sales is not collected, and which assets contribute most to turnover.

11. (d) The first three are true of the book value of equity.

12. (a)

13. (e)

14. (e)

15. (c) Banks are usually highly leveraged so they are likely to have high debt-to-equity ratios and low return on assets. They have no inventory so it's not strange for them to have a high inventory turnover ratio. However, it's not good for them to have a low return on equity.

16. (d)

17. (a)

18. (b) All of these statements are true, but B is the most important point of doing the case study.

Traditional Fundamental Analysis III: Earnings Analysis, Cash Analysis, Dividends, and Dividend Discount Models

CHAPTER 11

1. a. EBITDA—earnings before interest, taxes, depreciation, and amortization

   b. EBIT—earnings before taxes and interest

   c. Net income

   d. Net income available to common shareholders

2. True

3. Uncertain—this is often true, but it depends on the actual event.

4. Uncertain—long-term stock returns are related with accounting (reported) earnings, but it's not clear whether they are also correlated with true earnings.

5. False—other events in the market can cause earnings surprises to be largely ignored.

6. (c) It uses net income (minus dividends for preferred shareholders) for earnings, and it is usually reported alongside EPS in financial statements.

7. (a) Research does not support the first and third statements.

8. (c) While the third statement is possibly true, no evidence of it is given.

9. Net Income = $5 million + $4 million + $6 million + $10 million
   = $25 million

There are no preferred shareholders so it's all available to common shareholders.

$$\text{EPS} = \text{Earnings to common/Shares outstanding}$$
$$= \$25 \text{ million}/\$5 \text{ million}$$
$$= \$5 \text{ per share}$$

10. P/E = Market price per share/EPS = $100/$5 = 20

The earnings yield is the inverse or $5/$100 = 5%

One can also calculate P/E using future estimated earnings.
Estimated EPS next year is $35 million/$5 million = $7
P/E = Market price per share/EPS = $100/$7 = approximately 14.1
The earnings yield is the inverse or $7/$100 = 7%

11. One can use diluted earnings per share. One can also take the earnings per share over several historical periods.

12. (e) All are used to measure a company's cash flows.

13. (b)

14. (d)

15. (a)

16. (c) The third statement would be an explanation for why the ratio is going up.

17. (b)

18. a. There is a weak relation between dividend yield and subsequent 10-year dividend growth.

    b. The dividend yield does not forecast future dividend growth.

    c. The dividend yield does predict future stock returns.

19. (b) The current market price is not necessary and neither is the ratio of dividends-to-earnings (dividend payout ratio).

20. a. There is no way of knowing when the market price will move to its fair price as predicted by the model.

    b. It doesn't tell us how mispriced the stock is relative to transaction costs.

    c. It fails to look at stock selection in the context of portfolio analysis, and instead looks at stocks in isolation.

21. The CAPM says that Return = Risk-free rate + Beta × Market risk premium.

    $$\text{Discount rate} = 3\% + 1.5 \times 6\% = 3\% + 9\% = 12\%$$

22. Price = $2/(1.12) + \$2.10/(1.12)^2 + \$2.205/(1.12)^3 + \$25/(1.12)^3$
    = $22.82

23. Price = $D_1/(r-g) = \$2/(0.12 - 0.05) = \$2/0.07 = \$28.57$

24. In four years, the dividend will be $2 \times (1.05)^3 = \$2.31525$
    Price after three years = $D_4/(r-g) = \$2.31525/(0.12 - 0.05) = \$33.08$
    The stock will be underpriced in three years.

25. Fair value = $D_4/(r-g) =$ Market Price
    $2.3125/(0.12 - g) = \$25$
    $g = 2.75\%$

26. $P = (D_0[1 + (p_U - p_D)g])/(r - (p_U - p_D)g)$
    = $2[1 + (0.6 - 0.3)\,0.05]/(0.12 - (0.6 - 0.3)\,0.05) = \$19.33$

27. a. Dividends don't actually grow at a constant rate so the fair value from using the model may be off significantly.

b. If the growth rate is greater than the discount rate, the model fails.

28. True

29. True

30. False—market value almost always deviates from the fair value predicted by all the different dividend discount models.

CHAPTER 12

Security Analysis Using Value-Based Metrics

1. (b)

2. Net profits = (EBIT − Interest − Taxes)
   = (550 − 380 − 40 − 30 − 10 − 36) = $54,000

   The firm is generating a positive accounting profit.

3. NOPAT = EBIT × (1 − t) = (550 − 380 − 40 − 30) × (1 − 0.4)
   = $60,000

4. Pretax debt cost = Interest/Long-term debt = $10,000/$100,000 = 10%
   After-tax debt cost = Pretax debt cost × (1 − t) = 10% × (1 − 0.4) = 6%

5. Cost of equity = Risk-free rate + Market risk premium × Beta
   = 3% + 8% × 1.5 = 15%

6. WACC = Weighted debt cost + Weighed equity cost
   = (1/3 × 6%) + (2/3 × 15%) = 2% + 10% = 12%
   $WACC = WACC × C = 0.12 × $300,000 = $36,000

7. EVA = NOPAT − $WACC = $60,000 − $36,000 = $24,000
   Thus, the firm is also generating a positive economic profit as well as a positive accounting profit.

8. ROC = NOPAT/CAPITAL = $60,000/$300,000 = 20%
   RROC = ROC − WACC = 20% − 12% = 8%

9. Firm value = Capital + NPV = $300,000 + 5 × $24,000 = $420,000

10. (c) Adding equity can help to increase EVA only if the firm has positive growth opportunities.

11. (e) All three are special accounting adjustments that help improve the approximation.

12. (d)

13. (a) CFROI is a value-based metric and it is not a dollar-based measure.

14. (c)

15. True

16. True

CHAPTER 13

Multi-Factor Equity Risk Models

1. Statistical significance

2. (b) Historical alpha has almost nothing to do with volatility

3. (b)

4. a. Common factor risk versus stock-specific risk

   b. Systematic (market) risk versus residual risk

   c. Active risk versus benchmark risk

5. The largest risk factor bet is on momentum.

6. The three largest industry bets are in semiconductors (+11.564%), electronic equipment (+5.86%), and securities/asset management (+3.888%).

7. The three largest sector bets are in technology (+23.38%), telecommunications (−5.00%), and consumer cyclicals (−4.66%).

8. (b)

9. (e) All three are drawbacks of multi-factor models.

10. True

11. False—exposures to risk factors are in units of standard deviation and exposures to industry factors are in percentages.

Equity Derivatives I: Features and Valuation

1. 1-g, 2-i, 3-a, 4-f, 5-d, 6-h, 7-b, 8-c, 9-e

2. a. Risk management—to modify the risk characteristics of a portfolio.

   b. Returns management—to enhance the expected return of a portfolio.

   c. Cost management—to reduce transaction costs associated with managing a portfolio.

   d. Regulatory management—to achieve efficiency in the presence of legal, tax, or regulatory obstacles.

3. (c) OTC markets provide more flexibility.

4. (b)

5. (d) The contract value of an index option is the index value times a multiplier.

6. (a)

7. False—there is no actual boundary on the loss of a call option writer because the price of the underlying asset can indeed be very high.

8. True—as the option goes deep into the money, the price of the option becomes (almost) linear and loses (almost) all curvature. Another way of seeing this is that as the option goes deep in the money, the delta doesn't change at all (it's almost one and it cannot go above one), so the change in delta over a change in the price of the underlying is zero.

9. True—put-call parity allows us to use a call option fair value to find out the fair value of a put option with the same expiration and strike price.

10. False—there are circumstances under which it is preferable to exercise prior to the expiration date so an American option should be worth more than a European option.

11. The intrinsic value right now is $0 because she could buy the stock cheaper on the market. The difference between the price and the intrinsic value is the time value. Thus, the time value of the contract right now is $400.

12. The intrinsic value is now ($102 – $100) × 100 = $200. The rest is time value so that equals $600 – $200 = $400.
Delta is the change in price of the option over the change in price of the underlying,

$$(\$6 - \$4)/(\$102 - \$98) = 0.5$$

13. The intrinsic value of the option is now ($105 – $100) × 100 = $500 There is no more time left so the time value is zero. The price of the option is thus $5 per share. Her profit is $5 – $4 = $1 × 100 shares = $100.

14. a. Spot price of the underlying asset

  b. Strike price

  c. Time remaining till expiration date

  d. Expected price volatility over the life of the option

  e. Short-term interest rate over the life of the option

  f. Anticipated cash dividends on the underlying asset over the life of the option

15. (c) Lower interest rates would cause the option value to decrease.

16. (b) The other two measures can cut either way, but the time to expiration will always go down and it is always preferable for an option to keep its time value for a longer period of time.

17. They're marked to market on a daily basis. This means that every day's gains or losses are immediately settled. As a result, one can only default on one day's losses, and maintenance margin is used to prevent this from happening.

18. The six-month dividend yield is $1.02^{0.5} - 1 = 1\%$

    The six-month borrowing rate is $1.06^{0.5} - 1 = 2.96\%$

    Theoretical futures price $= 1,500 \times [1 + 0.0296 - 0.01] = \$1,529$

19. Borrow $1,500 at the 6% annual lending rate. Purchase $1,500 of the index-replicating portfolio. Sell the futures at $1,550. After six months, you will receive $15 (or 1%) in dividends from the cash portfolio and settle the short futures position by delivering the index to the buyer for $1,550. From the $1,565 in proceeds, you must repay the loan + interest = $1,500 + $44 (or 2.96%) = $1,544. This leaves $21 in risk-free profit.

20. a. Netting Arrangements between counterparties specify that in the event of a default, the bottom line is the net payment across all contractual agreements.

    b. Position limits are implemented depending on a counterparty's creditworthiness and other positions.

    c. Collateral is sometimes required in the form of liquid short-term assets.

    d. Recouponing is the changing of the coupon to make sure that the marked-to-market value of the position is zero.

    e. Credit trigger provisions allow a party to have the position settled in cash if the counterparty's credit rating falls.

    f. Derivatives product companies maintain high credit ratings.

21. (d)

22. (c)

CHAPTER 15

Equity Derivatives II: Portfolio Management Applications

1. (e) All of the statements are true.

2. (c)

3. a. Cost management—the synthetic position may be more cost-effective than the cash position

   b. Evading regulations such as those that prevent some companies from holding short positions

4. (b)

5. (a) Hedge ratio = $0.5 \times 1.1 = 0.55$

6. Equivalent market index units = $10,000,000/800 = 12,500
   Beta-adjusted market index units = $12,500 \times 0.55 = 6,875$
   Number of contracts = $6,875/100 = 68.75$ contracts

7. Then the appropriate hedge ratio is just the portfolio beta which is 0.5

8. (b) Synthetic index funds have lower costs than real index funds. The investor doesn't have control over portfolio constituents in either case.

9. a. Changing the portfolio composition to take advantage of superior stock selection or sector selection skills.

   b. Doing stock index arbitrage to take advantage of mispricing in the futures market.

   c. Using a structured product like an equity swap with leverage to increase returns.

10. True

11. True

12. False—the opposite is true. An in-the-money call behaves more like a stock and thus has a lower beta than an out-of-the-money call.

13. (a) A protective put has an expected return below the risk-free rate because it acts as insurance.

CHAPTER 16

Fixed-Income Securities

1. 1-d, 2-j, 3-e, 4-h, 5-k, 6-c, 7-g, 8-a, 9-i, 10-b, 11-f, 12-l

2. (c) $10,000 × 6% = $600. Semiannual is half of $600 = $300.

3. (e) All are false. Call provision is worse than no-call provision. Refunding protection is worse than call protection. Early first call date is worse than late first call date.

4. (b) Both the call protection and the put provision have value for the investor which is reflected in a higher price of the bond.

5. (d) Treasury bills are issued at a discount and have no coupon rate.

6. (a) 20 coupons (10 years of semiannual coupons) plus the principal payment

7. (b) Neither Freddie Mac securities nor municipal bonds are backed by the full faith and credit of the U.S. government. TIPS are issued by the U.S. Treasury.

8. True

9. Uncertain—a hard put means that the bond must be redeemed with cash, and a soft put means that the bond can be redeemed with cash, securities, or a combination of the two.

10. The stated conversion price equals the par value divided by the conversion ratio.

$1,000/40 = $25

11. No.
The value of the shares (after option is exercised) is the conversion ratio times the market price.

$$40 \times \$28 = \$1,120$$

The market value of the bond (which is $1,200) exceeds the value of the stock so there is no point of exercising. The investor can simply sell the bond in the market for $1,200 and buy the same amount of stock for $1,120 and still have $80 left over.

12. a. Character of management—includes analyzing management's strategic direction, financial philosophy, conservatism, track record, succession planning, and control systems.

b. Capacity to repay obligations—includes analyzing industry trends, the regulatory environment, competitive position, financial position, sources of liquidity, company structure, and special event risk.

c. Collateral—includes analyzing assets pledged to secure debt and analyzing the quality and value of other unpledged assets.

d. Covenants—includes analyzing the terms and conditions of the lending agreement.

13. (a) They do not only have AAA ratings (those are called prime) and they are less safe than U.S. Treasuries which are essentially immune from default.

14. (b) Municipal bonds can be taxable, and they are not necessarily guaranteed by state revenues and may thus be at risk of default.

15. a. Insured municipal bonds are backed by insurance policies written by commercial insurance companies. The insurance companies agree to pay any due principal or interest on a maturity date that has not been paid the by the bond's issuer.

b. Bank-backed bonds are supported by certain types of credit that are provided by commercial banks. These include letters of credit, irrevocable lines of credit, and revolving lines of credit.

c. Some municipal bonds are refunded when the source of the cash payments becomes bonds guaranteed by the U.S. Treasury instead of tax revenue. The bonds are usually then called at the first possible call date.

16. (c)

17. a. Auto loan-backed securities are securities whose cash flow depends on scheduled monthly interest and principal payments on car loans.

b. Student loan-backed securities are securities whose cash flow depends on student loan payments.

c. SBA loan-backed securities are securities whose cash flow depends on payments on small business loans.

d. Credit card receivable-backed securities are securities whose cash flow depends on credit card payments.

e. Collateralized debt obligations are backed by a diversified pool of junk bonds, emerging market bonds, and/or bank loans to corporations.

18. (e) The first two affect the discounted cash flows of the instrument; the last one affects the level of prepayments.

19. (c) The credit rating of the lenders is irrelevant because they do not owe anything.

20. a. A corporation may guarantee protection against losses.

b. A bank may offer a letter of credit to protect against losses.

c. Bond insurance may be used to guarantee protection against losses.

d. Reserve funds from issuance proceeds or excess servicing spread may be deposited into a fund to protect the bondholders.

e. The security may be overcollateralized so that a cushion exists to protect the bondholders in case of small losses.

f. A senior-subordinated structure may be formed so that the lower tranches absorb initial losses.

CHAPTER 17

Real Estate-Backed Securities

1. 1-e, 2-i, 3-d, 4-h, 5-b, 6-f, 7-a, 8-j, 9-c, 10-g

2. (f) The monthly interest payments are not fixed in dollar terms. They decline as the principal gets paid off. The monthly principal payments are not a fixed percentage of the remaining principal. Instead, they increase in both dollar and percentage terms. As a result, the principal repayment process accelerates (i.e., not in a linear fashion) as the mortgage approaches the maturity date.

3. (a) Low PTI and low LTV offer the least chance of default.

4. Because the annual mortgage rate is 6%, the monthly rate is 1/12 of 6% = 0.5%. Thus, the interest portion of the first payment is 0.5% × $200,000 = $1,000. The remainder of the $1,193 monthly payment must go toward principal. $1,193 − $1,000 = $193

5. During the last payment, the remaining mortgage balance must be paid out. We can designate that as P. The interest portion of the last payment is 0.5% of P. Thus, we can write the following equation:

$$P + 0.005P = \$1,193$$

Solving this leads to Principal = $1,187.06 and the remainder is thus interest: Interest = $5.94.

6. (a) Only Ginnie Mae mortgages are guaranteed by the federal government. Also, not all mortgages in a pool have the same maturity, which is why the weighted average maturity (WAM) is calculated.

7. (e) All the statements are true.

8. Because the annual WAC is 9.75%, the monthly WAC is 1/12 of 9.75% = 0.8125% Thus, gross interest paid in the first month is 0.8125% × $500,000,000 = $4,062,500. The passthrough rate is 9%, the monthly passthough rate is 0.75% and the monthly net interest is 0.75% × $500,000,000 = $3,750,000. The remainder of $312,500 is paid in servicing or other fees.

9. CPR = 6% × (25/30) × 1.20 = 6%

10. SMM = $1 - (1 - 0.06)^{1/12}$ = 0.5143%

11. Prepayment = SMM × (Beginning Balance – Scheduled Payment)
    = 0.5143% × ($500,000,000 – $336,290) = $2,569,777

12. Payment = (Share) × (Net Interest + Principal + Prepayment)
    = (12/10,000) × ($3,750,000 + $336,290 + $2,569,777)
    = $7987.28

13. (d)

14. a. Refinancing to take advantage of lower interest rates

    b. Moving to a new house

15. False—the opposite is true. A prepaid penalty mortgage reduced the risk for prepayment. As a result, it is worth more (higher price) or returns less (lower coupon).

16. False—that would be the average life of a passthrough. The WAM is the average maturity of the mortgages in the pool weighted by the outstanding balance on each mortgage.

17. Uncertain—It depends on the fixed mortgage rate in the contract and the prior path of interest rates.

18. True

19. (d) Lower interest rates lead to more prepayments and a lower discount rate. The latter is a positive effect.

20. a. In a sequential-pay CMO, one class of bond is completely retired before principal begins to be repaid on the next class.

  b. In accrual bonds, at least one tranche doesn't receive current interest payments. Instead, the interest amount is added to the principal balance and the money is used to repay the principal of earlier tranches.

  c. In planned amortization class CMO tranches, if prepayments are within a certain range, the cash flow is known for the PAC tranches. The prepayment risk is thus absorbed by the other tranches, known as support or companion tranches.

21. (c) The accrual tranche reinvests all principal and interest at the mortgage rate so if interest rates drop, nothing needs to be reinvested at these lower rates until all the other tranches are fully paid off.

22. (e)

23. (e)

24. a. Pool insurance is a form of external credit enhancement used to cover losses resulting from default and foreclosure.

  b. The shifting interest mechanism is a mechanism that allocates prepayments in such a way that the credit protection for the senior tranche is not eroded over time.

25. a. Prepayment lockout is an agreement that prevents prepayments over a specified period of time.

  b. Defeasance means that rather than directly prepaying a loan, the borrower must provide sufficient funds for the servicer to invest in a portfolio of Treasuries that would replicate the cash flows that the lender would have received in the absence of prepayment.

  c. Prepayment penalty points are predetermined penalties that the borrower must pay in order to refinance.

  d. Yield-maintenance charges make it uneconomical for the borrower to refinance solely to get a lower mortgage rate.

26. True

27. True

CHAPTER 18

General Principles of Bond Valuation

1. a. Estimate the expected future cash flows.

   b. Determine the appropriate rates to discount each of the cash flows.

   c. Calculate the present value by adding up the discounted cash flows.

2. (e)

3. (b) Treasury Bills are issued as discount securities and don't pay a coupon.

4. a. The level of benchmark interest rates

   b. The risks that the securityholder is exposed to

   c. The compensation the market expects to receive for those risks

5. We can use the semiannuity formula for the coupons and add the present value of the principal payment to get the total value.

   Semiannual coupon rate = 5%, Semiannual discount rate = 4.5%
   Present value of annuities = $5 \times (1 - (1/1.045^{10}))/0.045 = \$39.57$
   Present value of principal = $100/1.045^{10} = \$64.39$
   Price = $39.57 + $64.39 = $103.96

It trades at a premium because it is offering a coupon rate that is higher than current interest rates so investors are willing to pay more to hold it.

6. $100: When coupon rate equals the yield required by the market then the price is equal to the par value.

7. The number of days between settlement date and the next coupon date equals $183 - 109 = 74$. So $w = 74/183 = 0.404$ periods until next coupon.

Now we calculate the present value of all the cash flows.
For example, the first coupon's PV is $\$5/1.045^{0.404} = \$4.91$
The second coupon's PV is $\$5/1.045^{1.404} = \$4.70$
We add up all the discounted cash flows to obtain the full price $= \$106.72$

8. The accrued interest is the semiannual coupon payment $\times (1 - w)$:

$$AI = \$5 \times (1 - 0.404) = \$2.98$$

This needs to be subtracted from the full price to obtain the clean price:

$$\text{Clean price} = \$106.72 - \$2.98 = \$103.74$$

9. a. The first reason is due to an accounting convention: Since we subtract the value of the undiscounted accrued interest from the full price instead of the discounted accrued interest, we are subtracting too much, which makes our value lower than it should be in the marketplace.

   b. The second reason is that the price of a bond that is selling at a premium always decreases over time even when interest rates remain unchanged. This is known as pull to par value.

10. (a) Prices and discount rates are not linearly related. Also, when interest rates rise, bond prices decrease (not increase) at a decreasing rate.

11. Each security only pays the par value at maturity.

For the 6-month T-bill, the price is $100/(1.012) = \$98.81$
For the 1-year T-bill, the price is $100/1.0145)^2 = \$97.16$

12. The 1.5-year T-note makes 3 coupon payments of $1.65 and a final principal payment of $100. Each cash flow has to be discounted at the appropriate discount rate.
Price = $1.65/(1.012) + 1.65/(1.0145)^2 + 101.65/(1 + r)^3 = \$100$
We can solve this to get $r = 1.655\%$ and the annual spot rate is $2 \times r = 3.310\%$

13. The 2-year T-note makes 4 coupon payments of $1.75 and a final principal payment of $100. Each cash flow has to be discounted at the appropriate discount rate.

$$\text{Price} = 1.75/(1.012) + 1.75/(1.0145)^2 + 1.75/(1.01655)^3 + 101.75/(1 + r)^4 = \$100$$

We can solve this to get $r = 1.756\%$ and the annual spot rate is $2 \times r = 3.512\%$

14. (b) Since the par curve is upward sloping, spot rates are higher than yield to maturities (as in the previous two questions). Thus, strips are returning less than they should. They should be sold short and Treasuries should be bought.

15. False—Strips are not as liquid as Treasuries (they have higher liquidity risk), their tax treatment is different, and they give special advantages to non-U.S. investors. Thus, their rates won't be the same as the theoretical spot rates.

16. True

CHAPTER 19

Yield Measures and Forward Rates

1. a. The periodic interest payments

   b. Any capital gain or capital loss when the bond matures or is sold by the investor, or is called by the issuer

   c. Income earned from reinvestment of a bond's interim cash flows

2. The income earned from reinvestment of bond's interim cash flows depends on future interest rates and is thus unknown. Coupon payments and capital gains or losses are known when the bond is held to maturity.

3. The total dollar return if coupons can be reinvested at 8% is just the total future dollars minus the price paid for the bond.

   Total future dollars = $100 \times (1.04)^6 = \$126.53$

   Total dollar return = $\$126.53 - \$98.25 = \$28.28$

4. The periodic interest payments equal $6 \times \$4 = \$24$
   The capital gains equals $\$100 - \$98.25 = \$1.75$
   The reinvestment value can be obtained by using the formula for the future value of an ordinary annuity.

   Reinvestment income = $\$4 \times [((1.04)^6 - 1)/0.04] - \$24 = \$2.53$

5. Current yield is equal to the annual coupon payment divided by market price.

$$\text{Current yield} = \$8/\$98.25 = 8.14\%$$

6. We are looking for the semiannual yield which makes the two sides of the following equation equal:

$$\$98.25 = \$4/(1 + y) + \$4/(1 + y)^2 + \$4/(1 + y)^3 + \$4/(1 + y)^4$$
$$+ \$4/(1 + y)^5 + \$104/(1 + y)^6$$

Using trial and error, we get a semiannual yield to maturity of 4.3375% and a bond-equivalent yield to maturity of 8.675%.
This yield is greater than the current yield because the current yield ignores the built-in capital gain if the bond is held to maturity.

7. The bond's total future dollars would be $\$98.25 \times (1.043375)^6 = \$126.76$

$$\text{Total dollar return} = \$126.76 - \$98.25 = \$28.51$$

8. The answer in question 7 is different from the answer in question 3 because yield to maturity assumes that coupons are reinvested at the yield to maturity of 8.675%. However, we initially specified that the coupons would be reinvested at the coupon rate of 8%. This difference in the assumed reinvestment rate leads to the $0.23 discrepancy, and is a product of reinvestment risk.

9. (c) Bonds with a lower maturity and a lower coupon rate (with the same yield to maturity) have the lowest reinvestment risk.

10. False—the yield on a portfolio is the internal rate of return on the total cash flows of the portfolio. It is not a simple weighted average but is affected by other factors such as the different maturities of the constituents.

11. True

12. Uncertain—this statement is true only if investors don't demand a risk premium for holding long-term bonds, and if investors' preference for positive convexity doesn't influence the yield curve.

13. (d)

14. The implicit forward rate can be found by the following formula:

$$[(1.0534)^{15}/(1.05)^{5}]^{(1/10)} - 1 = 5.51\%$$

15. Since the forward contract rewards you with a better rate than the implicit forward rate, it's possible to make a profit by borrowing for 15 years at 5.34%, lending for five years at 5% and entering a forward contract to lend for the 10 years after that at 5.6%.

You lend at $(1.05)^{5} \times (1.056)^{10} = 2.2$

$$2.2^{(1/15)} = 5.397\%$$

You borrow at 5.34%.
The annual arbitrage profit is 5.7 basis points.

16. (a) An upward sloping spot yield curve only tells us about implied forwards. It doesn't necessarily tell us about market expectations or what future interest rates will actually be.

CHAPTER 20

Valuation of Bonds with Embedded Options

1. (d) The issuer is short the bond; the investor is short the call.

2. (b) The issuer is short the bond; the investor is long the put.

3. (f) The first and second statements are true for both spreads. (For zero-volatility spreads, the volatility is constant at zero.) The third statement is false for both spreads.

4. (d) For putable bonds, the option cost is negative which means that the option-adjusted spread is greater than the zero-volatility spread.

5. The formula is: Standard Deviation = $r_0\sigma$

$$0.65\% = 5\% \times \sigma$$
$$\sigma = 13\%$$

6. The sigma can be found by the following formula: $r_{1H} = r_{1L} \times e^{2\sigma}$

   Using the values in the table: $5.642\% = 5.105\% \times e^{2\sigma}$
   $\sigma = 5\%$

7. The following table illustrates the prices/cash flows from this bond.

Today	Year 1	Year 2	Year 3	Year 4	Year 5
				$97.398	$100
				($5)	($5)
			$95.378		
			($5)		
		$94.661		$98.074	$100
		($5)		($5)	($5)
	$95.148		$96.638		
	($5)		($5)		
$96.726		$96.372		$98.693	$100
		($5)		($5)	($5)
	$97.201		$97.799		
	($5)		($5)		
		$97.955		$99.261	$100
		($5)		($5)	($5)
			$98.867		
			($5)		
				$99.780	$100
				($5)	($5)

The theoretical value of this bond is $96.726.

8. The following table illustrates the prices/cash flows from the putable bond. When a value (except in year 1) is less than $98, it is replaced by the put value of $98, and the new value is used for calculations in all previous years. Replaced values are shown in bold.

Today	Year 1	Year 2	Year 3	Year 4	Year 5
				$97.398 ($5)	$100 ($5)
			$95.657 ($5)		
		$96.528 ($5)		$98.074 ($5)	$100 ($5)
	$97.499 ($5)		$96.638 ($5)		
$98.241		$97.108 ($5)		$98.693 ($5)	$100 ($5)
	$98.022 ($5)		$97.799 ($5)		
		$98.051 ($5)		$99.261 ($5)	$100 ($5)
			$98.867 ($5)		
				$99.780 ($5)	$100 ($5)

The theoretical value of the putable bond is $98.241.

9. The value of the put option for the investor is the value of the putable bond minus the value of the option-free bond.

$$\text{Put value} = \$98.241 - \$96.726 = \$1.515$$

10. (b) Higher volatility causes the value of the option to increase.

11. (d) Option-adjusted spread strips out from the nominal spread the amount that is due to option risk.

12. (b) Whether it's positive or not depends on the risk of each corporation. As in question 11, the option-adjusted spread strips out from the nominal spread the amount that is due to option risk. It does however, include compensation for liquidity and firm-specific credit risk.

13. (e) All three are necessary for a Monte Carlo simulation.

14. True

15. False—simulated interest rates are also necessary as inputs into a refinancing model to be able to simulate mortgage refinancing rates. These determine the future cash flows.

16. False—support tranches face more prepayment risk and thus have a higher nominal spread than the senior tranches.

Measuring Interest Rate Risk

1. a. Term to maturity

   b. Coupon rate

   c. Level of yields

   d. Presence of embedded options

2. (b) The longer the average maturity of the cash flows (modified duration), the more price is sensitive to yield changes. Long maturity and zero-coupon have the longest duration.

3. (e) All are true for option-free bonds.

4. (d) Putable bonds exhibit price compression at high yields as their price approaches the put strike price. They have no regions of negative convexity, unlike callable bonds, which have negative convexity at low yields.

5. (a) If its call option is out-of-the-money, it means that the loan rate is below current interest rates. As a result, it is in a region of positive convexity and it's also not very likely to be prepaid (unless the borrower decides to move).

6. Duration = $(V_- - V_+)/2V_0(\Delta y)$ = $(101.574 - 98.456)/(2 \times 100 \times 0.002)$
   = 7.795

7. Duration $= (V_- - V_+)/2V_0(\Delta y) = (108.176 - 92.561)/(2 \times 100 \times 0.01)$
   $= 7.808$

8. There is no significant difference because for option-free bonds, the magnitude of the rate shock has very little impact on the calculation. For more complicated bonds, the chosen rate shock may affect the calculated duration.

9. Approximate price change $= -$duration $\times \Delta y \times 100$
   $= -7.795 \times 0.02 \times 100 = -15.59$

   Estimated price = Current price + Price change
   $= \$100 - \$15.59 = \$84.41$

10. The actual price is higher because duration always underestimates the true price. (In this case, it is actually \$85.79.)

11. Its yield to maturity is the value that makes $\$100/(1 + y)^2 = \$94.26$
    That value is 3.0%.
    The Macaulay Duration is $(2 \times PVCF_2)/Price = 2$

12. The modified duration is the Macaulay Duration/$(1 + $ yield$) = 2/(1.03) = 1.942$

13. Its maturity equals its duration.

14. Duration of a portfolio is just the weighted duration of the portfolio's parts.

    Duration $= [(50,000/90,000) \times 6] + [(40,000/90,000) \times 8] = 6.89$

15. The contribution of the first bond is $(50,000/90,000) \times 6 = 3.33$
    Thus, even though it is more than half of the portfolio in market value, it is less than half of the portfolio's exposure to interest rate changes.

16. This can be accomplished by selling the entire \$40,000 of the second bond and \$5,000 of the first bond. The \$45,000 in cash can then be used to buy a bond with a duration of 4. The duration of the portfolio will then be $[(45,000/90,000) \times 6] + [(45,000/90,000) \times 4] = 5$
    There are other ways that this can be accomplished such as, for example, selling all the bonds in the portfolio and investing the \$90,000 in an issue with duration of 5.

17. They have the same duration so they have equal exposure to parallel movements in the yield curve.

18. The long part of the yield curve is likely to move up, causing the yield curve to become upward sloped. Bond A has more exposure to the long part of the yield curve and is likely to decline by more.

19. (C) A 5-year bond is not affected by the 30-year key rate movements nor can it have a duration of 9.

20. Convexity = $(V_- + V_+ - 2V_0)/2V_0(\Delta y)^2$

    Convexity = $(101.574 + 98.456 - 200)/(2 \times 100 \times 0.002^2) = 36.816$

21. Convexity adjustment = Convexity $\times (\Delta y)^2 \times 100$
    $$= 36.816 \times 0.02^2 \times 100 = 1.47$$

    Adding that to the value we obtained in question 9:

    Estimated price = Duration-estimated price + Convexity adjustment
    $$= \$100 - \$15.59 + \$1.47 = \$85.88$$

22. For option-free bonds, they are positively convex everywhere so the convexity adjustment is always positive. Another way to look at it is that the duration always underestimates the true value for option-free bonds, so the convexity adjustment has to be positive to bring it closer to the true value.

23. The PVBP is the decrease in value of the bond if its yield rises from 5% to 5.01% (or equivalently, the increase if the yield falls to 4.99%).

    Estimated price = Current price – Duration adjustment
    + Convexity adjustment

    Estimated price = $\$100 - [\text{Duration} \times \Delta y \times 100] + [\text{Convexity} \times (\Delta y)^2 \times 100]$
    $$= \$100 - [7.795 \times 0.0001 \times 100]$$
    $$+ [36.816 \times 0.0001^2 \times 100]$$
    $$= \$99.9221$$

    Thus the PVBP is $\$100 - \$99.9221 = 7.79$ cents

24. True

25. False—Interest rate risk also depends on the yield volatility.

CHAPTER 22

Fixed-Income Portfolio Strategies

1. a. Interest rate risk is the risk that the security's price will change as a result of a change in the general level of interest rates.

   b. Yield curve risk is the risk that the security's price will change as a result of a change in the shape of the yield curve.

   c. Call (or prepayment risk) is the risk that the expected cash flows will not occur because a bond is called or mortgages are prepaid.

   d. Credit risk is the risk that the issuer will not make the expected interest or principal payments or the security's price will fall because of worsening credit quality.

   e. Liquidity risk is the risk that the investor will have to sell at a bad price because of low liquidity (high bid-ask spreads).

   f. Exchange rate or currency risk is the risk that the cash flows from foreign bonds will not be worth as much in domestic currency because of exchange rate depreciation.

2. (b) U.S. Treasuries are noncallable, they are considered default-free, they are extremely liquid, and they are traded in dollars.

3. (d) It is exposed to interest rate risk and yield curve risk because it is a fixed-income security. It is callable so it is exposed to call risk. It is French, so U.S. investors are exposed to exchange rate risk. It may

not be very liquid so it is exposed to liquidity risk. It is AAA but it may be downgraded so it is also exposed to some credit risk (in the form of credit spread risk and downgrade risk).

4. a. Default risk is the risk that the issuer will be unable to meet contractual interest or principal payments.

   b. Credit spread risk is the risk that the market will demand a higher credit spread (and thus a lower price) for a security as the issuer's financial health deteriorates.

   c. Downgrade risk is the risk that a security will fall in price because it is downgraded by a rating firm.

5. (d) The employee doesn't need to buy or sell any securities in the marketplace (because they can be held to maturity) and thus is not worried about liquidity risk at all. The other three have different levels of exposure to liquidity risk.

6. We use the future value of an annuity formula from Chapter 19 to get the value of the coupons in two years. The annual reinvestment rate is 4.8%.

Coupons and reinvestment income = $2.5 \times [(1.024)^4 - 1)/(0.024)]$
$$= \$10.37$$

Total future dollars = $103 + $10.37 = $113.37

Semiannual total return = $(\$113.37/\$100)^{1/4} - 1 = 3.19\%$

Bond-equivalent total return = $3.19\% \times 2 = 6.38\%$

Effective rate total return = $(1.0319)^2 - 1 = 6.48\%$

7. The bond-equivalent return is the right return to use for such a comparison because returns on bond benchmarks are usually calculated by doubling the semiannual return (i.e., on a bond-equivalent basis).

8. (e) All three are necessary inputs for total return calculations.

9. a. Scenario analysis involves calculating the total return for a small number of possible scenarios to test the sensitivity of a certain input variable on the total return.

   b. A Monte Carlo simulation involves giving probability distributions to all the input variables and performing a large number of trials to determine the probability distribution of the total return.

10. (d) The first is not true. An indexing strategy is likely to be inappropriate for meeting liabilities because the returns on the index are unlikely to be related to the cash flows necessary for the liability.

11. (c)

12. (e)

13. (a) A leveraged portfolio is more sensitive to changes in interest rates and, as a result, has a higher duration.

14. (b)

15. a. The static return is the return that would be earned if there was no interest rate volatility. It can be decomposed into the risk-free return and the accrual of OAS return.

    b. The interest-sensitive return is the return that is due to changes in the level, slope, or shape of the yield return. It can be decomposed into effective duration return and convexity return.

    c. The spread-change return is the return that is due to changes in sector spreads and the spreads of individual securities. The portion attributable to changes in the OAS spread is called the delta OAS return and the portion due to changes in the spreads of specific issues is called the delta rich/cheap return.

    d. The trading return is the return that is due to changes in the composition of the portfolio.

    e. The residual is the difference between the total return and the return attributable to the four factors above.

16. (d) There is no proper frequency for rebalancing. Rebalancing involves a trade-off between transaction costs and ensuring that the duration is the right one.

17. (a)

18. True

19. True

CHAPTER 23

Bond Portfolio Analysis Relative to a Benchmark

1. The portfolio has a higher exposure to corporate securities than the index. They make up one half of the portfolio's market value and only one third of the index's market value. The portfolio is also more sensitive to movement in corporate securities because the contribution to duration is 2.60 for the portfolio and only 1.93 for the index.

2. The portfolio is underweighting both the short and long end of the yield curve, and instead is overweighting bonds whose adjusted durations are in the middle (between 3 and 7 years).

3. The large mismatches in both sector weights and duration weights suggest that this portfolio is actively managed with a large leeway given to the manager in making bets on duration and credit spreads.

4. (d) The first is false. Under the cell-based comparison, it is simple to calculate the difference in exposures or contribution to duration and use those as quantifiers of a mismatch.

5. a. The cell matching (stratified sampling) method involves making sure that for all cells, the benchmark index and the portfolio have similar weights. The holdings of securities in a particular cell are usually computed to match that cell's contribution to overall duration.

   b. Tracking error minimization uses a multi-factor risk model to minimize tracking error for a fixed number of securities. Obviously, it is easier to obtain lower tracking error with a larger portfolio, but tracking error minimization achieves the optimal level of tracking error for any chosen portfolio size.

6. (b)

CHAPTER 24

Multi-Factor Fixed-Income Risk Models and Their Applications

1. (e) All three are uses of a multi-factor risk model

2. (c) Passive managers use risk models to choose securities to minimize tracking error.

3. a. The tracking error summary report breaks down tracking error related to each cross-sectional comparison. Thus, it allows the portfolio manager to determine the sources of the total tracking error.

   b. The set of risk sensitivity reports compares the portfolio composition to the composition of the benchmark and allows the manager to see what mismatches are leading to the total tracking error for each individual source.

4. (b) Concentration risk is diversifiable (by adding more securities) and is thus a nonsystematic risk.

5. False—the mismatches can cancel out as a result of the correlation structure. Thus, cash flow mismatches don't necessarily translate into tracking error.

6. False—it depends on the correlations, but usually the tracking error of the whole is not the sum of the tracking errors of the parts.

7. True

8. Contribution = $\sqrt{12 \times (0.0159 \times 0.0023)^2}$ = 0.00040

So Bond A contributes approximately 4 basis points.

9. Contribution = $\sqrt{12 \times (0.0916 \times 0.0023)^2}$ = 0.00073

So Bond B contributes approximately 7.3 basis points.

10. a. One way to minimize a portfolio's tracking error from nonsystematic sources is by having very small mismatches in weights.

b. A second way to minimize a portfolio's tracking error from non-systematic sources is by choosing securities with low issue-specific volatility.

11. (d)

12. (a) The difference between sigmas is usually not equivalent to the tracking error.

13. a. A risk model can be used as a diagnostic tool to quantify the risk of a portfolio. In this way, one can evaluate the achieved return of a portfolio relative to the level and kinds of risk that it was exposed to, and use that to grade the risk-adjusted performance of the manager.

b. A risk model can be used to project the effect of a proposed transaction on the tracking error. Thus, passive managers can use it to make transactions that do not alter the portfolio's risk profile, but achieve lower tracking error.

c. A risk model can be used for portfolio optimization with minimum turnover. The input into the model is the universe of available assets. The model is used to search for transactions that will minimize the portfolio's tracking error. The final output is a list of the best (lowest-cost) transactions that will optimize the tracking error.

14. False—active managers can optimize their portfolio by lowering their risk profile in some areas while keeping exposure in other areas where they want that exposure.

15. Uncertain—it depends on the definition of risk. For passive managers, for example, tracking error risk is more important than absolute risk (which is the risk measured by sigma).

Fixed-Income Derivatives and Risk Control

CHAPTER 25

1. a. Forwards only

   b. Futures only

   c. Both

   d. Forwards only

   e. Futures only

2. (c) The delivery must be made using one of a few bonds that the CBOT has approved.

3. Invoice price = Contract size × Futures price × Conversion factor

   Invoice price = $100,000 × 1.025 × 0.9102 = $93,295.50

4. The purchase price of the Treasury bond is $92,625. The sale price (for the short) is $93,296. The profit is $93,296 − $92,625 = $671. The 60-day implied repo rate is $671/$92,625 = 0.724%

5. Invoice price = Contract size × Futures price × Conversion factor

   Invoice price = $100,000 × 1.025 × 0.9263 = $94,945.75

The purchase price of the Treasury bond is $93,969. The sale price (for the short) is $94,946. The profit is $94,946 – $93,969 = $977.
The 60-day implied repo rate is $977/$93,969 = 1.04%

6. The cheapest-to-deliver is the issue that gives the highest implied repo rate. The second issue has a repo rate of 1.04% while the first issue only has an implied repo rate of 0.724% so the second issue is cheaper to deliver.

7. (b) A lender would want to buy Treasuries and sell futures. The implied repo rate would be the return on the loan.

8. (f) All the options in a futures contract are options of the short position, not the long position.

9. (d)

10. a. The cost of carry model assumes there are no interim cash flows. In fact, interim cash flows need to be reinvested and the reinvestment rate affects the futures price.

    b. The theoretical price assumes the borrowing and lending rates are equal. In reality, the borrowing rate exceeds the lending rate so there is actually a range of arbitrage-free prices.

    c. Thirdly, the cost of carry model does not account for the value of the delivery options of the short position. Thus, it overestimates the true value of the futures contract.

11. (b) Eurodollar CDs actually are denominated in dollars. They are also settled in cash. The third statement, however, is true, as Eurodollar futures are used to lock in a future 3-month rate.

12. a. Transaction costs are lower for trading futures.

    b. Margin requirements are lower for futures which permits greater leveraging.

    c. It is easier to sell short in the futures market than in the Treasury market.

13. If the price change from a 100 basis point movement in rates is $9 million, the percentage move is $9 million/$150 million = 6%, so the

portfolio's duration = 6. The portfolio exceeds the client specified exposure.

14. By selling futures, it is possible to reduce duration to 4 (or equivalently reduce dollar duration to 4% × $150 million = $6 million).

15. The dollar duration of one futures contract = dollar duration of the CTD issue × conversion factor for the CTD issue:

$$= \$4,200 \times 1.04 = \$4,368$$

Number of contracts = (Target dollar duration − Current dollar duration)/
Dollar duration per futures contract
= ($6 million − $9 million) / $4368 = −686.8

The manager should sell approximately 687 futures contracts.

16. True

17. False—the value of the fixed payments received by the floating-rate payer changes with changing interest rates.

18. (a)

19. (c) The dollar duration of a swap for a floating-rate payer is equal to the dollar duration of a fixed-rate bond. The dollar duration of the floating-rate bond is close to zero and it can be ignored.

20. a. The first assumption is that the price can take on any positive value with some probability. In fact, the value of bonds can not exceed the sum of all principal and coupon payments unless negative interest rates are allowed.

    b. The second assumption is that the short-term interest rate is constant. This is completely inappropriate for securities whose price changes with changing short-term interest rates.

    c. Thirdly, the Black-Scholes model assumes that volatility is constant over the life of the option. However, the volatility of bonds decreases as they approach maturity.

    d. The appropriate method for valuing options on fixed-income securities is the arbitrage-free lattice method.

21. The difference between strike price and the interest rate is 1%. The payment is thus equal to 1% × 0.25 × $5 million = $12,500

22. Zero. The interest rate is above the strike rate so a floor doesn't pay anything.

23. a. Credit options pay only if an event occurred or if the credit spread is above or below a certain strike price.

    b. Credit forwards have a payout that depends on the difference between the credit spread at settlement and the credit spread in the contract.

    c. Credit swaps allow an investor to exchange the cash flows from a risky security for certain known cash flows from the counterparty.

24. (b) A portfolio that is properly hedged against credit risk only suffers from counterparty risk.

CHAPTER 26

Investment Companies

1. (b) The price of mutual funds is always equal to the NAV. This is different for closed-end funds which can trade at a discount or premium to NAV.

2. NAV = Market value/Shares outstanding
   = $300 million/20 million = $15 per share

3. NAV = Market value/Shares outstanding
   = $320 million/20 million = $16 per share

   The new deposits of $8 million are bought for $16 per share so a new 500,000 shares are issued.

   Shares outstanding = 20 million + 0.5 million = 20.5 million shares

   However, this deposit doesn't change the NAV.

   NAV = Market value/Shares outstanding
   = $328 million/20.5 million = $16 per share

4. (d)

5. (a)

6. (c) There are mutual funds that invest only in bonds as well.

7. a. A front-end load is deducted from the initial investment amount.

b. A back-end load is charged at the time that fund shares are sold. The most common back-end load is a contingent deferred sales charge. In this system, the back-end load that would need to be paid upon withdrawal gradually decreases over time.

c. A level load is a constant load that is charged every year.

8. (c) Sophisticated investors usually do not purchase mutual funds with loads.

9. (d) An actively managed emerging markets fund would probably be most difficult to mange and would probably have the highest expense ratio.

10. (d) Front-end loads are not a part of the annual expense ratio.

11. a. Mutual funds reduce the cost of eliminating nonsystematic risk through diversification.

b. Mutual funds reduce the costs of contracting and processing information because of economies of scale.

c. Mutual funds are managed by supposedly professional managers who are more experienced and better qualified than most individual investors.

d. Mutual funds provide liquidity because they can be easily sold at the NAV without any bid-ask spreads.

e. There are a large variety of funds allowing investment by sector, asset class, and so forth.

12. (c)

13. (b) The Morningstar Rating System gives each company a number of stars but doesn't tell you their exposure to various groups. Newspapers usually only provide pricing data. The Sharpe Benchmark is the best way to determine exposures.

14. (a) Investors usually don't pay commissions on reinvested distributions, and the fact that closed-end funds trade below NAV hurts

investors when they sell but helps them if they buy shares on the open market. The lack of control of the tax burden is the biggest disadvantage of distributions.

15. False—load funds have not disappeared because many investors remain dependent on financial advisors' services and counsel.

16. True

17. Uncertain—this is usually true but for some passive funds, it is possible that distribution fees and other expenses can be more substantial than the management fees.

CHAPTER 27

Exchange-Traded Funds

1. (d) Program trading was the origin of the idea behind ETFs.

2. (f) All of the statements are false. SPDRS account for only one-third of ETF assets. TIPs were discontinued because they proved too costly for the exchange. There are now many ETFs that don't use the unit investment trust structure.

3. (c) WEBS were not the first ETFs traded on the secondary market.

4. (d) The creation/redemption processes do not prevent small investors from using ETFs by trading them on the secondary market.

5. a. ETFs are large so fixed costs are not as large a percentage of the total pie.

   b. In-kind transactions lower the fund's transaction costs.

   c. Shareholder accounting at the fund level has been eliminated.

6. (b) Long-term investors who do not trade often and who can take advantage of the ETF's tax efficiency would find it most advantageous.

7. (b)

8. (e)

9. (c) The first two factors contribute to tax efficiency of open-end ETFs. The third factor contributes to the tax efficiency of HOLDRs and Folios.

CHAPTER 28

Real Estate Investment

1. a. Private commercial real estate equity

   b. Private commercial real estate debt

   c. Public real estate equity

   d. Public commercial real estate debt

2. (c) Exhibit 28.1 in *The Theory and Practice of Investment Management* clearly shows that choices a, b, and d are not true.

3. a. Real estate is a debt/equity hybrid.

   b. The value of real estate rarely goes to zero because it is a physical asset.

4. (d) The other three assets behave more like equity.

5. (d)

6. a. Leases provide stable cash flows that are unrelated to shifts in the economy.

   b. Real estate is a debt-equity hybrid so the cross correlation between the two behaviors drives down the total volatility.

   c. There is a great range of different cycles across the country occurring simultaneously, so the private equity sector is fairly diversified, which reduces volatility.

7. (d) In exchange for adherence to certain rules, the income of REITs is not taxed at the corporate level, but only at the shareholder level.

8. (d) REITs are sometimes correlated with the stock market and sometimes they are not correlated. It largely depends on how private real estate is performing at the time.

9. a. Adding real estate reduces the overall risk of the portfolio by adding an uncorrelated asset class.

   b. Adding real estate can help boost the portfolio's absolute return.

   c. Real estate can help hedge a portfolio against unexpected inflation.

   d. Real estate can help passive investors achieve a portfolio that better reflects the entire investment universe.

   e. Real estate can deliver strong cash flows to the portfolio.

10. (c) Because real estate is a low-risk asset and acts to reduce both risk and return, it is not appropriate for investors who are looking to take high-risk gambles.

11. (b) Real estate debt is affected adversely by inflation because inflation causes nominal interest rates to rise. Publicly traded real estate equity is affected adversely by inflation because it is correlated to the stock market, which is itself hurt by inflation.

12. (e) All are useful for risk-sensitive investors.

13. (c)

14. True

15. False—the cost approach can be interesting for determining if new supply will appear, but it is practically useless in valuing real estate.

16. Uncertain—it depends on the time period and the measure of risk.

CHAPTER 29

Hedge Funds

1. a. The number and type of investors are limited for hedge funds while there is no such limitation for mutual funds.

   b. Hedge funds hold portfolios that are much more concentrated than those of mutual funds because they are not trying to meet any return benchmark.

   c. Hedge funds use derivative strategies often while mutual funds are usually limited in their use of derivatives.

   d. Hedge funds can buy and sell short securities while mutual funds can only decide either to buy or not buy. Furthermore, mutual funds can not hold large cash positions even if they expect a downturn, while hedge funds can move in and out of the market to time its movement.

   e. Hedge funds can use a large amount of leverage to multiply the small gains from arbitrage bets. Mutual funds are limited in their use of leverage.

2. 1-d, 2-b, 3-a, 4-g, 5-e, 6-f, 7-c

3. (b) In fact, the majority of long/short hedge funds do bottom-up analysis. They look for specific securities instead of first choosing the best industries.

4. (d) On the contrary, many global macro funds were able to profit from the devaluation of the British pound in 1992.

5. (e) Arbitrage funds usually try to eliminate most or all of their market exposure.

6. (d) In a sudden economic downturn, many planned mergers are canceled. This is a systematic risk of merger arbitrage funds because it can not be diversified away.

7. (c)

8. (a) Market timers usually use top-down strategies.

9. (a) Most hedge fund returns are positively (but not perfectly) correlated with the stock market. The big exception is short selling hedge funds. Research has not conclusively proven that hedge fund returns are or are not persistent.

10. False—because hedge funds are not highly diversified, their beta is not a good way of measuring their total risk. This is because beta does not measure the exposure of hedge funds to idiosyncratic or firm-specific risk.

11. True—arbitrage involves riskless profits.

12. False—because hedge funds are a relatively new instrument, many funds don't have a long enough track record to use as the sole criteria for selection.

13. a. Opportunistic hedge fund investing involves providing the investor with new investment opportunities that can not be obtained through long-only investment.

    b. Investing in a hedge fund of funds allows investors to gain the advantages of investing in a single hedge fund but eliminates the idiosyncratic risk of one fund manager.

    c. Absolute return investing involves using hedge funds to attain a certain target rate of return irrespective of the return from the market or other benchmarks.

14. a. A hedge fund manager should be able to explain the investment objective of the hedge fund.

    b. A hedge fund manager should be able to explain the investment process and how it achieves the objective of the hedge fund.

    c. A hedge fund manager should be able to explain their superiority to other managers.

15.

    a. Information filtering

    b. Information gathering

    c. Information filtering

16. (c)

17. True

18. False—black box processes can do as well or better than open processes, but there is a process risk to investing in hedge funds that don't publicize the process by which they expect to meet their objectives.

CHAPTER 30

Private Equity

1. (a) The first one is the typical company that receives venture capital.

2. (c) The main disadvantage of investing in any fund of funds is the extra layer of fees.

3. (d) Venture capitalists almost always receive senior equity stakes in the form of preferred stock.

4. a. The venture capital firm will analyze the business plan to determine whether the company's financial goals are attainable.

   b. The venture capital firm will make sure that all intellectual property rights are given up to the company, and that key employees sign agreements not to leave and join another competitor.

   c. The venture capital firm will analyze the equity stakes that are given to other companies, and will check the company's prior operations to make sure that there are no outstanding problems.

   d. The venture capital firm will review the resumes of all of the members of the management team to determine if it is able to implement the business plan.

   e. The venture capital firm will determine if the company requires regulatory approval for its products.

   f. The venture capital firm will check if there is any outstanding litigation against the company.

g. The venture capital firm will determine the likelihood and timing of an exit plan to turn the equity stake into a cash profit.

5. (e) All three should be found in a business plan

6. a. The venture capitalist can bring in more seasoned management professionals to run the company.

   b. The venture capitalist may provide legal or regulatory advice and help the company receive a patent for its technology or gain regulatory approval for a product.

   c. The venture capitalist may use its contacts with established companies or investment banks to enable the company to be acquired or go public.

7. True

8. True

9. False—the limited partnership is preferred when money is to be raised from a large number of passive investors.

10. a. Venture capital firms can specialize by industry.

    b. Venture capital firms can specialize by geography.

    c. Venture capital firms can specialize by stage of financing.

    d. Venture capital firms can specialize in "special situations," which usually means turnaround ventures.

11. Return on capital = $200 million/$1.6 billion = 12.5%

12. It must pay $400 million to debtholders and $1.2 billion × 1.2 = $1.44 billion to the equityholders.

    Total required capital = $1.44 billion + $400 million = $1.84 billion

13. Using the discounted cash flow model, the value of an annuity of $250 million discounted at 8% is $250 million/0.08 = $3.125 billion

14. The final value is $3.125 billion. The initial investment was $500 million.

Annual return = $3.125 billion/$500 million)$^{1/6}$ − 1 = 35.72%

15. The upside would be a much higher of rate of return. The downside would be that there is much lower room for error. If the cash flows could not meet the higher debt payments, the company would have to declare bankruptcy and the equityholders could lose everything.

16. a. The LBO firm can sell the company to a competitor.

b. The LBO firm can take the company public again.

c. A second leveraged buyout can be performed.

d. The company can reintroduce debt to pay a large dividend to the equityholder.

17. (a) Venture capital deals usually require less capital than leveraged buyouts, and leveraged buyouts are highly leveraged while there is usually little or no leverage in venture capital deals.

18. (e)

19. (c)

20. (b) Investors in mezzanine funds are generally pension funds, endowments, and foundations, not large individual investors.

21. (b)

22. (c) The price of distressed debt is not really affected by interest rates for the reason stated.

23. (d) Because distressed firms are already likely in default, credit risk is not really a risk of buying their debt. Instead, the company's business success will determine if the debt will appreciate in value.

24. True

25. False—mezzanine debt has returns that are typically lower than the returns on equity because it has debt-like aspects that bring down the rate of return.

26. False—usually distressed debt arbitrage is conducted by buying distressed debt and selling the stock.

CHAPTER 31

Active Asset Allocation

1. a. Both

   b. Tactical asset allocation

   c. Tactical asset allocation

   d. Policy asset allocation

   e. Tactical asset allocation

   f. Tactical asset allocation

2. (e) All are problems with optimization techniques.

3. (a) Volatility is not the only risk faced by investors and mean-variance optimization is not a necessary technique for accomplishing policy asset allocation.

4. a. On March 31, the portfolio will be rebalanced so that stocks again comprise 60% of the portfolio.

   b. The portfolio will be immediately rebalanced so that stocks comprise 64% of the portfolio.

   c. The portfolio will be immediately rebalanced so that stocks comprise 60% of the portfolio.

   d. No rebalancing will occur.

5. (b)

6. a. Asset allocation strategies must determine where the opportunities for superior returns lie, that is, where there are disequilibrium conditions.

   b. Asset allocation strategies must ascertain whether these markets can sustain a return to equilibrium.

   c. For global assets, asset allocation strategies must assess whether foreign capital will be drawn to these markets.

   d. They must consider whether the markets will move now or later.

7. (c) Tactical asset allocation strategies also can seek to participate in intermediate or long-term movements in asset classes.

8. a. Minimization of transactions costs

   b. Excellent liquidity and quick execution

   c. Simultaneous trading in different asset classes

   d. Does not disrupt management of underlying assets

   e. Income stream from underlying assets is unchanged

   f. Possible to take advantage of favorable mispricing of the futures

9. a. It is also possible for there to be unfavorable mispricing of the futures.

   b. There is extra administrative work because futures are marked to market every day and gains/losses have to be settled daily.

   c. A cash liquidity reserve is necessary to meet margin requirements.

10. False—portfolio insurance is a dynamic asset allocation strategy that synthetically replicates the performance of put options.

11. True

12. True

13. True